The
LLANELLY & MYNYDD MAWR RAILWAY

by
M.R.C. Price

THE OAKWOOD PRESS

© Oakwood Press 1992

ISBN 0 85361 423 7

Typeset by Gem Publishing Company, Brightwell, Wallingford, Oxfordshire.
Printed by Alpha Print (Oxon) Ltd, Witney, Oxfordshire.

Acknowledgments

Grateful thanks are due to all those mentioned below, and not least the
very helpful staff of a number of libraries and archives:

The Public Record Office; The House of Lords Record Office; The National
Library of Wales, Aberystwyth; The Dyfed County Record Office, Carmar-
then, and especially the County Archivist, John Owen; Llanelli Public Lib-
rary and the Borough Librarian, D.F. Griffiths; Swansea University Library;
British Rail, Swansea; Edinburgh Central Library; The Scottish Record
Office; The Bodleian Library, Oxford; The GWR Museum, Swindon, and
Thamesdown Borough Council; The Locomotive Club of Great Britain; The
National Railway Museum, York; Colonel Stephens Museum, Kent & East
Sussex Railway, Tenterden; The Historical Model Railway Society, and the
Industrial Railway Society.

R. ab Elis, H. Bassett, D. Bevan, R.E. Bowen, R.M. Casserley, D. Charles,
J.M. Clunas, R.A. Cooke, R.S. Craig, T. David, F. Davies, T. Davies,
W. Davies, J. de Haviland, G. Ebenezer, A. Ellis, P.V. Evans, M. Hale,
R. Harragan, F. Jones, R.P. Jones, R.W. Kidner, J. Lowe, Mrs M. Mainwaring,
D. Mansel Lewis, J. Miller, H.L. Morgan, R.L. Pittard, K.P. Plant, C.R. Potts,
the late P.G. Rattenbury, the late E.S. Rees, P.R. Reynolds, R.C. Riley,
K. Robertson, Mrs P. Slade, J.N. Slinn, Mrs H. Thomas, R.L. Thomas,
E.S. Tonks, N.T. Wassell, Welsh Railways Research Circle, E. Wilkins,
K. Winder.

Published by
The OAKWOOD PRESS
P.O.Box 122, Headington, Oxford.

Contents

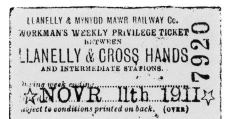

Courtesy Trefor David

Preface

The Carmarthenshire Tramroad and its lineal successors survived many vicissitudes for 186 years. The original enterprise had unique characteristics seldom acknowledged by railway historians. Although it was the second railroad in Britain to obtain an Act of Parliament, it was probably the first public railway to become operational, as Mr Connop Price suggests. Moreover, unlike most of the pioneering railroads, it was able to mobilise outside capital, and was surely the earliest known example of such an undertaking to engender a 'London Committee'. This sets it apart from other pioneer railways which relied much more significantly on local capital.

The original scheme owes its origins to the entrepreneur Alexander Raby who sought to develop ironworks and collieries in the Llanelli district: that he was able to raise capital and initiate the railway and its associated shipping place, signifies his drive and initiative. Unhappily, his blast furnaces could rely neither on local ironstone, nor the advent of peace in Europe for their success, and his colliery ventures never achieved anticipated sales.

As was often to be the case in west Wales, although many embarked capital in transport facilities and collieries, relatively few achieved a measure of success. Financial viability depended critically upon the quality of coal, and the ability to ship it cheaply and efficiently. These, in the local context, were conditions hard to meet, not least because many proprietors were undercapitalised and manifested a marked reluctance to embark in collaborative ventures such as good port facilities.

The promotion of the Llanelly & Mynydd Mawr Railway Company in the 1870s was a local initiative, and sought local finance, but without much success. It was a newcomer to West Wales, the Scotsman John Waddell, whose capital and expertise restored hope that the venture could attain prosperity. However, shipping facilities in the Burry Estuary were a constant constraint on coal sales and a financial burden on the local community. Trade prospects were never secure enough to generate the capital necessary to fund port facilities comparable with those offered by rival ports to the east of Llanelli. There was never much hope that Llanelli could attract the increasing size of shipping which characterised the second half of the 19th century. When new facilities were created, they were small in scope and too belated to succeed.

Against this background, Mr Connop Price has researched widely and has composed a narrative which is admirable in its scope and coherence. The story he tells is a complex interaction of rivalries, confusions, hopes and disappointments. On occasion, as with the long-lasting dispute between Waddell and the Llanelli Harbour Trust, there is an element of farce intermingled with tragedy, with so much at stake for local employment and prosperity. However, Mr Connop Price tells the story without the historian's all too glib assumption of wisdom after the events here recounted. He finds more to praise than to blame, despite the need to reassess old and painful controversies. His admiration for John Waddell is just, since he manifested both foresight, enterprise and determination. It is to be hoped that this study, and the efforts of local railway preservation enthusiasts, will serve to maintain some evidence of a past era, and that such efforts will form a memorial to an enterprise which contributed much to the industrial history of west Wales.

Robin Craig, B.Sc(Econ), F.R.Hist,Soc., late Senior Lecturer, Department of History, University College London.

Introduction

The town of Llanelli (known as Llanelly prior to 1966) stands on the north shore of the Burry Inlet, with views across the water to Penclawdd and the Gower peninsula. Unlike the Gower, however, Llanelli stands on an historic coalfield. Although mining was abandoned in the borough soon after World War II, the industry had its origins at least as early as the 16th century. Much of the history of the industry has been well described in the work of M.J. Symons, but in 1991 the only coal mines anywhere near the town are at Tumble and Cwmgwili (Cross Hands), near the head of the Gwendreath Valley. In spite of many difficulties, there is also a possibility of a new drift being opened at Carway Fawr, Cynheidre.

The early development of the coal industry in Llanelli and district undoubtedly discouraged many visitors. In 1821 the town was described in most unflattering terms as 'a miserable dirty place filled with miners and sailors'. The presence of coal was also a factor in the growth of both the steel and the tinplate industries at Llanelli; indeed in the 19th century the town was synonymous with tinplate. Now, apart from the Trostre works of British Steel, this has all gone. Most of the port facilities have been closed for almost 40 years, and the townspeople of Llanelli are looking to a very different future. Plans are afoot for the extensive redevelopment of South Llanelli, and if these schemes come to pass Llanelli's shoreline may be changed as dramatically in the 21st century as it was in the 19th, when industrial and port expansion pushed the coastline from Sandy down to the point below the North Dock.

Inland the scene is also changing. In the 19th and 20th centuries collieries and waste tips scarred the landscape of the Gwendraeth Valley, and also the upland area north of Llanelli known as Mynydd Mawr ('the Great Mountain'). Now much of the evidence of mining has been swept away, leaving former colliery villages like Pontyberem, Tumble and Cross Hands to find a greener future. Improved roads, and new routes like the Cross Hands by-pass, have enabled some residents of these villages to work right outside the area, but the Mynydd Mawr district is still substantially Welsh in language and culture. Whilst some older inhabitants retain fascinating memories of the Mynydd Mawr railway and the collieries it served, an entire generation has grown up with knowledge of little more than Cynheidre, the 'super pit' recently abandoned as much by the problems of politics as by the problems of geology.

Many local people have been generous with their time and their trouble in helping me to learn more of the Llanelly & Mynydd Mawr Railway, and its predecessor, the historic Carmarthenshire Railway or Tramroad. I am very pleased to thank everyone mentioned in the acknowledgements, whether local to the district or resident elsewhere. Some also deserve special mention, including my knowledgeable friend Ray Bowen, who was a companion on several visits to the line, and to the historian Robin Craig, formerly of Llanelli, for his thoughtful preface to this book, and for his helpful comment on the manuscript. Gordon Rattenbury and Paul Evans provided some very stimulating observations on the tramroad era, whilst Paul Reynolds, Michael Hale and Roger Kidner drew my attention to numerous other noteworthy points. Similarly I am most grateful for all the encouragement and support offered by Jane Kennedy and Colin Judge of the Oakwood Press, but I have to say that after all the good advice and assistance, responsibility for the manuscript is mine. Last, but by no means least, I must thank Judy, David and Katy for allowing me time over several years to pursue this project to completion. It would have been impossible without their help.

Martin R. Connop Price
Hook Norton, Oxfordshire
April, 1992

The Monmouthshire Railway Society's 'Robeston Rambler' tour at Cynheidre on 14th October, 1989. This was the last BR working over the former Llanelly & Mynydd Mawr railway.   *Author*

Chapter One
Prelude and Postlude

At about 11.30 am on Saturday 14th October, 1989, two 3-car diesel multiple units forming a Monmouthshire Railway Society railtour train, pulled out of the down platform of Llanelli station. A few hundred yards to the west, by Old Castle crossing, the train turned north onto the branch line running inland to Cynheidre colliery. A few spectators near the junction took photographs, and others waved. This was British Rail's last train over the remaining portion of the Llanelly & Mynydd Mawr Railway.

Alongside the branch at Old Castle lengths of flat bottom rail were visible in the grass, the last vestiges of the Stradey Estate line, otherwise known as the Mansel Lewis private railway. As will be seen, this line occupied the alignment of the L&MMR's historic predecessor, the Carmarthenshire Railway or Tramroad, for about a mile. Keeping to the east of the old private railway, the railtour train crossed the River Lliedi and a level crossing by the Old Castle Inn, to run alongside the remaining premises of the Old Castle Tinplate works, in the occupation of Dyfed Joinery Ltd. On the opposite side of the line the Old Castle Pond and the Peoples' Park provided no indication of the importance of this district in the early industrial development of the town. Even the site of Llanelli steelworks, closed as recently as 1981, was landscaped and green. Nearby a new road was being built across the track-bed of the former Burry Port & Gwendraeth Valley Railway branch near the site of Sandy Junction.

In 1989 it was almost impossible to imagine that Sandy had ever been the location for a locomotive shed, a wagon works and a marshalling yard. The railtour train passed slowly beneath Sandy bridge on the surviving single track and continued north past Stradey Park, the home of Llanelli Rugby Club, the legendary 'Scarlets'. Close at hand on the railway, the site of the first locomotive shed was no more than a small mound of grass and brambles. Another rugby pitch belonging to the Furnace Rugby Club occupied the site of the Cille (or Castle) colliery. Turning north-east the train left the route of the old Carmarthenshire line to take an alignment provided in 1880 for the L&MMR. Running in cutting around the south side of Furnace, the tour train almost came to a halt on the gradient behind Saron chapel. Alongside Pentrepoeth road it picked up a little speed, and the driver announced the train's presence by blasting 'Come to the cookhouse door, boys' on the horn. This succeeded in attracting some surprised expressions and more waves. Back on the old Carmarthenshire Railway route, the diesel multiple units made heavy weather of the steepening gradient, and seemed to struggle over Felin Foel level crossing, where the crossing warning lights were flashing, and the siren blaring. Grey smoke belched out of the power cars as the train passed within sight of Felin Foel's famous brewery, and took to the hillside above Adulam chapel. Only after clearing the town for the countryside did the train seem to move more easily.

From Felin Foel to the Cwm Lliedi reservoir in Swiss Valley a footpath runs alongside the Mynydd Mawr line, giving a reminder of the tramroad

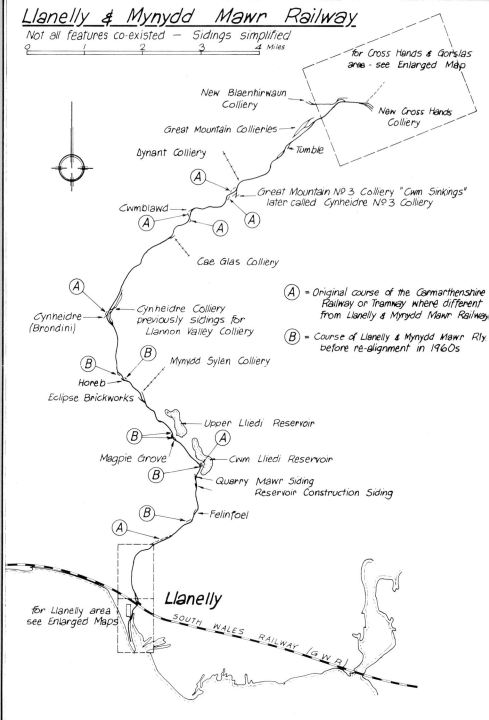

Llanelly & Mynydd Mawr Railway

Not all features co-existed — Sidings simplified

0 1 2 3 4 Miles

for Cross Hands & Gorslas
area - see Enlarged Map

New Blaenhirwaun
Colliery

New Cross Hands
Colliery

Great Mountain Collieries

Dynant Colliery

Tumble

(A)

Great Mountain Nº 3 Colliery "Cwm Sinkings"
later called Cynheidre Nº 3 Colliery

Cwmblawd

(A)

(A)

Cae Glas Colliery

(A)

(A) = Original course of the Carmarthenshire
Railway or Tramway where different
from Llanelly & Mynydd Mawr Railway

Cynheidre Colliery
previously sidings for
Llannon Valley Colliery

Cynheidre
(Brondini)

(B) = Course of Llanelly & Mynydd Mawr Rly.
before re-alignment in 1960s

(B)

(B)

Mynydd Sylen Colliery

Horeb

Eclipse Brickworks

Upper Lliedi Reservoir

(B)

(A)

Magpie Grove

Cwm Lliedi Reservoir

(B)

Quarry Mawr Siding
Reservoir Construction Siding

(B)

Felinfoel

(A)

Llanelly

for Llanelly area
see Enlarged Maps

SOUTH WALES RAILWAY (G.W.R.)

309

era, when the route was first a public right of way. After a warm, dry summer water levels were low in the Swiss Valley reservoirs in October, 1989. At Quarry Mawr the railway took the railtour away from the original course above Cwm Lliedi to pass through a deep rock cutting. Beyond there were glimpses of water through warm autumn leaves, whilst on the west side of the line trees crowded down by the track. The location of the 1960s loop at Magpie Grove was identifiable by an expanse of ballast on the west of the line, and a derelict concrete platelayers' hut. By now the mid-day sun was flickering through the carriages, and highlighting the gold and brown and red in the bushes and branches by the railway. Some cattle stampeded down a hillside at the unexpected sight of the train; there was the constant squeal of flanges against rails as the multiple units tackled a succession of reverse curves. It was a day for any enthusiast to relish.

Near Horeb an overgrown wall on the west of the line marked the site of the siding towards the ruins of the old Eclipse brickworks, presided over by a large red brick chimney. A short distance beyond, a small concrete loading platform was still in evidence in front of the chapel at Horeb. The train then picked up more speed to climb through woodland, and across damp moorland towards Cynheidre. South of the road overbridge, but within sight of the colliery, the railtour came to rest alongside sidings occupied by rolling stock belonging to the Llanelli & District Railway Society. As the colliery had closed over six months earlier, there was no activity near the mine, but the track and the sidings were littered with pieces of gleaming anthracite. There could be no mistaking the fact that the Mynydd Mawr line was intended to carry coal.

Running almost half an hour late, the railtour left Cynheidre for Llanelli at 12.22 pm. Had the passengers had time to follow the course of the railway further, they would have found that north of the colliery a half-mile section of track owned by British Coal had actually been lifted. They would also have discovered that a small underbridge south of Cwmblawd had been repaired, and that rusted rails remained in position to a loop north of Cwm, or. Cynheidre No. 3 colliery, originally linked with the Great Mountain complex. Only in the village of Tumble, a few hundred yards beyond, and at Cross Hands, had the L&MMR been entirely dismantled. Even in 1989 the Mynydd Mawr line still reached Mynydd Mawr, the 'Great Mountain', even though it had long been out of use beyond Cynheidre. Although there was some talk in October 1989, of retaining the track in case of future mining developments, the long career of the line as a commercial concern appeared to have come to an end. The story, as will be seen, had a history of almost two hundred years.

CARMARTHENSHIRE.

The Report of JAMES BARNES, *Engineer, as to the intended Rail Way or Tram Road, from the Flats, near* Llanelly, *to the Lime Rocks, near* Castle-y-Garreg.

I HAVE accurately measured the Length and ascertained the Acclivity, from tne Bay of *Llanelly*, to tle said Lime Rocks, and have found the Length to be Thirteen Miles Three Quarters, and the perpendicular Height, 847 Feet 11 Inches.—The Line of Country to be pursued, is in general favorable for a Rail Road, and abounds in good Materials for the Purpose, which lie convenient.

The Falls I have varied and proportioned in such a Manner, as will require no very great Exertion, for a Horse, to carry down Ten Tons.

A Road thus made, with Falls judiciously arranged and proper pass-by Places, will enable the Proprietors to carry on Business to any Extent, and the Country through which it passes holds out great Advantages, abounding with Veins of Coal, Culm, Iron Stone and Lime Stone.

The present improved State of Rail Roads, exhibits a Mode of Conveyance much superior to any Canal that is incumbered with a multiplicity of Locks, in a mountainous Country——It does not destroy half as much Land as a Canal, may be constructed for less than One Third of the Expence, (averaging Situations) requires no Reservoirs, no Water.——Its Trade suffers no interruption from excessive Drought in Summer, nor is it liable to any Inconvenience from Frost in Winter.

The easy Communication this Road will open through the Country, will be productive of the most bene ficial and interesting Effects, it will afford an easy Transit to the Port for all its different Commodities, and will encourage the Agriculture of the Country, by enabling the Farmer to purchase Lime at a much easier Expence than he can at present.

A constant supply of Coals being kept, at the Port of *Llanelly*, so that Vessels may depend upon quick dispatch, together with the superior Quality of these Coals will insure a Market, and an unlimited Trade.

I have estimated the Road, to be made 5 Yards Wide, and the Rails laid 4 Feet asunder, and I find it will require the Sum of £.18,467 16s. including the Bason and Wharf at *Llanelly* Port, all of which may be completed in the course of Twelve Months from passing the Act.

The probable annual Trade to be expected as soon as this Road is completed.

STANDS AS FOLLOWS:

	£.	s.	c.
FIRST,			
CARRIAGE of Coal and Culm, 20 Swansea Weys, or 260 Tons per Day averaging its Carriage 8 Miles, at 1½ per Ton per Mile	3000	0	0
II. Suppose Lime and Lime Stone, for Farmers' Use, to be conveyed only 2 Miles on each Side of the said intended Road, it would comprehend 50 Square Miles of Ground, or 32000 Square Acres, calculating that the Farmer limes only One Acre in every Ten, at 10 Ton per Acre, will amount to 32000 Tons, and averaging the Carriage at 6 Miles on the said intended Road, at 1½ per Ton per Mile, will amount to	1200	0	0
III. There are Two Iron Furnaces already built near the Flats, at *Llanelly*, which will be supplied with Iron Stone and Lime Stone along the said intended Road, and which at present consume as much Iron Stone and Lime Stone, as will pay the intended Rail Road, for Carriage per Annum	800	0	0
IV. The Back Carriage will consist of Binding Coals for Smiths and House Use, Pig Iron and Coals, for Two established Iron Works at *Llandevane*, which at a moderate Computation, cannot be estimated at less per Annum, than	500	0	0
	£.5500	0	0

SEPTEMBER 25, 1801.

James Barnes.

PRINTED BY J. VOSS, MARKET-PLACE, SWANSEA.

A reproduction of the *Report* of James Barnes, Engineer, for the proposed Carmarthenshire Railway, 1801. *Welsh Industrial and Maritime Museum*

Chapter Two
The Carmarthenshire Railway in the Raby era

In the year 1796 a wealthy Englishman, Alexander Raby, who owned copperworks at Penrhiwtyn (near Briton Ferry) and collieries at Neath, took over an iron furnace constructed at Cwmddyche (Furnace) by John Givers and Thomas Ingman in 1793. Raby may well have had an interest in the venture from its inception, but now he was determined to develop it to the full. He is said to have come with the sum of £175,000 raised from the sale of an estate at Cobham, Surrey. There is no doubt that he was soon committing his money wholeheartedly to industrial developments at Llanelly.

In March 1797, Dame Mary Mansell, owner of the Stradey estate, granted Raby a 91 year lease allowing him to work certain coal seams beneath the estate to the west of the river Lliedi. The lease was a long and complex document, intended not only to secure a good income for the estate, but also to ensure improved facilities for the coalfield. Accordingly Raby agreed to mine at least 1,000 weys of coal (approximately 5,000 tons) per year, at a royalty of two shillings per wey. Failure to mine this amount gave rise to a penalty of a similar sum per wey under the thousand. Amongst other things, Raby was obliged to supply coal free for use at Stradey Castle and to give compensation for agricultural land damaged by tipping. Most significantly the lease specified that Raby must provide a shipping place on the seashore, and a means of transport to reach it.

In spite of these somewhat restrictive terms, in January 1798, Raby obtained two further leases from the Stradey estate. By one he gained rights for 91 years to further coal seams west of the Lliedi at a royalty of three shillings per wey. He also agreed to set up a steam engine to facilitate deep working, and to pay after three years a minimum royalty of 3,000 weys (approximately 15,000 tons). The coal was almost certainly intended for export because this document was entitled 'Lease of the shipping colliery'. The second lease was for just 21 years, and covered lands on the west of Llanelly which enabled him to begin construction of his own tramroad to connect his coal and ironworks with his new shipping place on the mudflats at Llanelly. It is believed that part of the route of Raby's 'new iron way' was built with Dame Mary Mansell's consent on the alignment of an even earlier waggonway which had linked the Caemain pit with what was then the beach at Sandy.

Improved transport facilities were undoubtedly needed. Although there were several small 'shipping places' in existence, a common means of loading coal into ships at Llanelly was to beach them on the mudflats if they were small (under about 30 tons) or to use lighters or barges to ferry coal out to larger vessels anchored off-shore. Clearly this was extremely tedious, and costly in terms of time, labour and broken coal. The obvious solution was to build wharves so that coal could be loaded directly from wagons or drams into ships. One of the first such wharves at Llanelly was built in 1795 to serve a canal from pits owned by William Roderick, Thomas Bowen and Margaret Griffiths. This was later developed as the Pemberton's Dock. Alexander Raby's dock, or shipping place, was a short distance to the north-west, and it became known as the Carmarthenshire Dock. This dock and the tramroad serving it came into use by 1799. The most notable feature of the

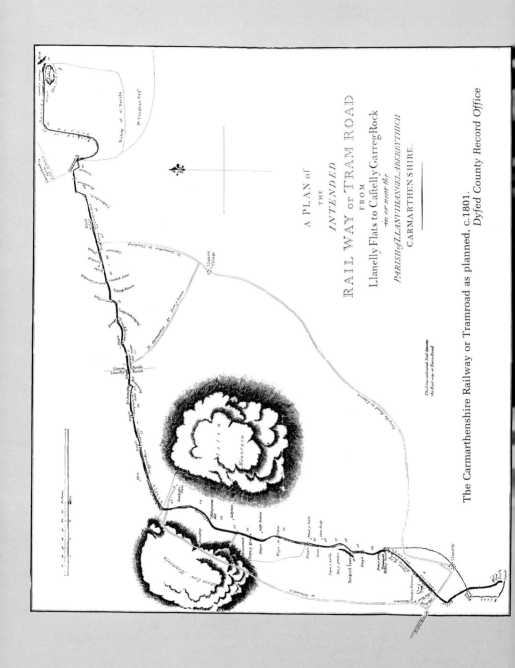

A PLAN of
THE
INTENDED
RAIL WAY or TRAM ROAD
FROM
Llanelly-Flats to Calfelly-Garreg-Rock
in or near the
PARISH of LLANVIHANGEL.ABERBYTHICH
CARMARTHENSHIRE.

The Carmarthenshire Railway or Tramroad as planned, c.1801.
Dyfed County Record Office

Two notable figures in the history of the Carmarthenshire Railway – Alexander Raby and R.J. Nevill.   *Llanelli Public Library*

A researcher measures stone blocks on the route of the Carmarthenshire Railway near Gorslas, in the summer of 1991.   *T. Davies*

tramroad was an iron bridge over the River Lliedi at Sandy, which is believed to have been the world's third iron railway bridge.

Raby worked quickly to develop his industrial empire, sinking a number of pits including that at Caemain, where his new steam engine was erected. Meanwhile his ambitions extended beyond the collieries at Llanelly and the ironworks at Cwmddyche. It was widely believed that Mynydd Mawr and the other hills inland would prove to be an El Dorado for minerals. Raby was determined to exploit these riches for the benefit of his industrial interests. He, and a number of others, looked keenly for ways of opening up the inaccessible areas of Mynydd Mawr. In the years 1790, 1793 and 1801 schemes were put forward for the construction of canals, the last two being well away from Llanelly, roughly following the course of the modern M4 and A48 from the River Loughor up to Cross Hands. It was soon realised that an immense amount of engineering and expense would be required to lift a canal into these hills, and it appears that in 1800 Raby initiated an alternative scheme to build a railway or tramroad from Llanelly to Mynydd Mawr – in effect extending his existing line to Cwmddyche.

In April 1801, the Burgesses of Llanelly gave their consent for the new undertaking to make rail or tramroads over Morfa Bach Common (Sandy). Preparations continued, and on 14th September, 1801, one Rhys Davies wrote from Swansea to potential supporters of the scheme:

> Several of the principle [sic] proprietors of land, coal and iron stone as well as the proprietor of the Iron Works and others considerably interested in the parishes of Llanelly, Llanon and Llanarthney, having thought a Public Iron Railway might materially contribute to the general advantage by the easier and cheaper carriage of coal, iron and lime stone to the Iron Works and the Port of Llanelly, a meeting is thought desirable on the subject to take place at Llanon, on Friday the Twentyfifth day of September instant at one o'clock, where the favour of your company is required.

It seems that some of the supporters soon invested money in the scheme, because on Thursday 5th November, 1801, at the Kings Head Inn, Llanon, there was a 'Meeting of the subscribers of the Intended Rail Road or Tramway from the Flats near Llanelly to Castell-y-Garreg.' This first recorded meeting of subscribers was chaired by Dame Mary Mansell's husband, E.W.R. Shewen. It was noted that the railroad and dock would be of 'great Public Utility', and it was resolved to seek an Act of Parliament for the construction of the line. A vote of thanks to Raby was passed, and he declared that he would use only limestone from Castell-y-Garreg at his ironworks.

The Act authorising the Carmarthenshire Railway or Tramroad was passed on 3rd June, 1802, (42 George III cap.lxxx), being only the second Act of Parliament promoting a public railway (independent of a canal) in Britain, the first being that for the Surrey Iron Railway in 1801. The share capital comprised £25,000 in £100 shares, together with power to raise up to £10,000 in loans secured against the company's assets. In addition to Raby, no less than 56 other subscribers were named. The Act empowered the company to acquire Raby's dock and tramroad system, and provided for the extension of the line to Castell-y-Garreg, some 3½ miles west of Llandybie.

The Carmarthenshire dock, Llanelly (note vessels on the slip behind).

Llanelli Public Library

Traffic in general merchandise as well as minerals was anticipated, and the Act specified that these be charged at a rate of 1½d. per ton/mile. Horses, mules and the like, (other than those employed on the railway) were subject to a toll of 2d. per head per mile, whilst cattle were charged 1d. per head per mile. Sheep, pigs and calves were 8d. per score per mile. For use of the dock a ship had to pay 1d. per registered ton, whilst all goods whether imported or exported were liable to a handling charge of 1d. per ton. The Act also specified that a hundredweight be 120 lb. rather than 112 lb. for the purpose of assessing tolls. Although the Weights and Measures Acts already declared a ton to be 2,240 lb., the difference here reflected the need to ensure that the customer received the full weight for which he was paying. Accordingly loads would be dispatched by the 'long ton', which allowed 8 lb. per hundredweight for any breakages in transit.

The Carmarthenshire's Engineer was named James Barnes, and it has been assumed that he was one and the same man as the James Barnes who worked with William Jessop on the building of the Grand Junction Canal. This cannot be taken for granted. It appears more probable that at the start of the 19th century there were two engineers named James Barnes. It has been suggested to the writer that one was born in 1740, and worked on several canals in the Midlands, including the Grand Junction, between 1799 and 1805. The other man, it is suggested, was active west of the Severn, and was probably younger. He was a contractor on the Penydarren Tramroad in September, 1800, and two months later was involved in a preliminary survey for the Sirhowy Tramroad. By 1801 he was Engineer to the Carmarthenshire Railway or Tramroad.

Unfortunately it is not known if James Barnes, the Midlands canal engineer, ever had a son with the same name. If true, this would provide a simple explanation for the activity of James Barnes in very different areas at the same time. It might also go some way to explain why the Engineer of the Carmarthenshire Railway used construction methods comparable to those of Benjamin Outram, who built a tramroad at Blisworth on the Grand Junction Canal. Many years later evidence of these methods was provided by correspondence discovered in an old desk belonging to Col. Buckley of the Buckley brewing family. Letters from an unnamed old retainer written to James Buckley at Bryncaerau Castle gave much new information.

He stated that 'the railway plates were laid on stone blocks one yard apart a hole bored in each stone a plug of wood in the hole and a nail driven to the plug to fasten two plates together'. However there is also evidence that after 1804 the fastening of the tramplates may have used a spikeless method devised by an employee of the Carmarthenshire company named Charles Le Caan. His tramplates were cast with a mortise at one end and a tenon at the other to ensure accurate alignment between plates. In addition a spigot or pin was cast into each end for insertion into wooden plugs in the holes bored in the stone blocks. The provision of this spigot or pin made separate spikes unnecessary. In 1807 this invention brought Le Caan a prize of 20 guineas from the Society of Arts, but in view of the old retainer's recollection of the spiked method it must be doubted if Le Caan's system was used very extensively.

The gauge of the Carmarthenshire Railway is also open to some debate. James Barnes' report of September 1801 clearly states his intention that the line should be built with 'Rails laid 4 Feet asunder'. In November 1805, the company decreed that 'no wagon should pass over the railroad having a greater gauge than 4 ft 4⅝ in. over the *outside* of the wheels.' Once again, however, the old retainer's comments have to be noted. Writing to James Buckley he said 'The Mynydd Mawr Railway was made 2 in. broder [sic] as far as Tyishaf Farm for convenience of coals from the Old Ship. [The Old Slip, near Furnace] He added 'The way we maniage was Take off and put on washers on the axeltry to width of 2 inches'. Although the writer stated that 'The Carmarthenshire Railway was the first of its length made in Wales', he also averred that there were railways at Llanelly before the Carmarthenshire 'and they were broder as far as Sandy Iron Bridge 2 inches than Mr Raby's Py'. On the assumption that 'Mr Raby's Py' means Raby's plateway and sidings, it would seem that the Carmarthenshire line was built to match the gauge of Raby's line, rather than the others, and that re-gauging wheels only became necessary at a much later date, probably after Raby's influence in Llanelly had waned, and that of the Nevill family had increased. On this basis it may be supposed that the old retainer's evidence relates only to the 1820s, by which time the several tramroads in Llanelly controlled by the Nevills had become dominant, causing the gauge of the Carmarthenshire below Tyisaf to be altered to correspond with them, that is to about 4 ft 2 in. Although the brevity of the retainer's evidence is a difficulty, there seems little doubt that the original gauge was 4 feet.

Construction proceeded apace, and in May 1803, the line was open for traffic from the ironworks at Cwmddyche down to the sea, a distance of one and a half miles. This short length of line thereby can claim to be the first public railway in use in Britain, because the better known Surrey Iron Railway, engineered by William Jessop, was not ready for traffic until July 1803. By that month Barnes was able to report that the first five miles of the Carmarthenshire, together with certain branches, were already in use. In addition, a further 6½ miles had been formed and awaited the laying of rails. Only the last 1¼ miles were untouched.

Such progress was a considerable achievement, because by tramroad standards the earthworks were substantial. For ease of handling by horse-power the gradients had to be minimized (the most severe gradient is believed to have been 1 in 38) and numerous embankments and deep cuttings were created on the sinuous line. By November 1803, the railway was open to Brondini (Cynheidre), some six miles inland and 500 feet above sea level. North of this point the railway was built close to the 500 foot contour, which eased the gradients but not the curvature of the track. Construction was slowed, however, partly by a preference to spend capital in Llanelly and partly by the need to build an immense embankment on Mynydd Mawr. This embankment, comprising 40,000 cu. yds of spoil was eventually completed by November 1804, and in the following year the line was open to Gorslas, Cross Hands. By then all the company's capital had been spent, and although in July and September 1807, the company adver-tised for someone to complete the railway, the last portion to the quarries at Castell y Garreg was never built.

During excavations for the line four outcrops of 'stone coal' (anthracite) were exposed near Cynheidre. Accordingly on 4th February, 1804, *The*

Cambrian of Swansea reported that the coal on the Brondini estate had been let to 'a respectable company of gentlemen', a group which included Raby's brother-in-law, Thomas Hill Cox. A week later *The Cambrian* advertised the Cynheidre colliery to be available to let for a term of years 'comprising several veins of stone coal and culm of the most approved quality, workable by level at an easy expence'. The advert also stressed the proximity of the colliery to a turnpike road and the Carmarthenshire Railway or Tramroad. The significance attached to the new line was further emphasized in the following month when a farm within 3 miles of Llanelly, and within a few hundred yards of the Carmarthenshire Railway, was reported to be for sale. If any doubt remained, the value of the railroad was demonstrated in June 1804, when it was announced that 'the valuable veins of Brondiny coal and culm have found their way to market by means of the Carmarthenshire Railroad. Such mode of conveyance bids fair to outrival, in point of regularity and terms, any canal in the Kingdom'.

In Llanelly the company pressed ahead with dock improvements. Raby's dock was reconstructed as the Carmarthenshire dock, and most of the new facilities were opened in 1804. Other work was completed in the following year, by which time additional improvements were being considered. The most substantial improvement was the provision of a 155 yds-long western arm to the dock, opposite Raby's original eastern wharf, the two being connected by a wall at the landward end. This enabled the tramroad to serve loading shoots on both sides of the dock. Although the wharfage was much increased, the new arrangements did not provide adequate protection against heavy seas.

Under the 1802 Act the company was empowered to make rules and regulations governing the operation of the line and the dock. The Carmarthenshire Railway was a true tramroad: the company provided the transport facility, and those using the line provided wagons approved by the company. Every wagon (spelt 'waggon' in the Act) had to carry a number, and the name and address of the owner. The company was entitled to measure or gauge up each wagon four times a year. The owners of wagons, or of vessels in the dock, were made liable for any damage caused by their possessions, and obstructions caused either by wagons or vessels could attract a penalty 'not exceeding five shillings nor less than one shilling for every hour such obstruction shall continue' after the making of a request for its removal. Likewise any person creating an obstruction was liable to prosecution, and anyone wilfully damaging, destroying or stealing any part of the 'Tramroad, Dock or Bason' could be tried as a felon – giving rise to the ominous possibility of transportation by way of penalty.

To what extent these rules had to be enforced is not known, but the old retainer who corresponded with James Buckley highlighted the problem of derailments. Many plateways suffered from broken plates, but he may have been speaking of the common problem of spreading track when he wrote: 'When the wagon goes over the plates (it was often the case) the weels at once was between two stone blocks impossible to get the wagon to the plates without epty the coal'. He added with feeling 'Many times it try my temper, but I don't recolect swearin as I herd many'.

The retainer noted that the distance by road from Furnace Gate to 'Gunhidre Colliery' was 4½ miles and over the railway 7 miles. The journey was slow and the loads light, each wagon taking just two tons (one later authority refers to 3 tons). 'One man and 2 Horses', wrote the retainer, 'takes 2 days to bring 4 tons of coals from Mynydd Mawr to the dock and back. Farmers from the neighbourhood of Gunhidre were the carriers. About half the way they might stop at home over the night and finish the journey next day'. In another letter the retainer stated that he had once done something no one else had done on the railway: 'On Mr. Buckley's request I made three journeys in one day to finish a small vessel before neptide. I had 12 Tons of Coals to fill and 12 empty with a shovel and 54 miles to travel'. The stated mileage indicates that the return journeys were not over the whole length of line to Gorslas, but probably no further north than Cynheidre. Even so, it was clearly a prodigious feat!

If, under these circumstances, the writer had felt the need to hurry down the steeply graded line, a braking system had already been considered. As early as 1798 Charles Le Caan had devised a system for tramroads with severe gradients which presupposed that the horses would be connected to the wagons by shafts, as on farm carts. In the ordinary way a horse would provide the brake power, but if a horse then fell, causing the shafts to drop, shoes attached by a chain automatically provided a braking action along the ground. However, as the notion of hitching horses to coal trams or wagons by shafts soon went out of favour, it must be supposed that this invention had a short life.

The 1804 annual meeting of the Carmarthenshire Railway or Tramroad Company was adjourned several times, and eventually took place on 31st January, 1805. The delay was explained by E.W.R. Shewen, Clerk to the company, as being due to the desire 'to inform subscribers that the Road is

The village of Furnace, as seen in an Edwardian postcard.   *Author's Collection*

finished to the foot of the Great Mountain (from which place, the principal part of the limestone will be brought) and within two miles of the intended termination at the Lime Rock'. To encourage further financial support Shewen added a statement of the railway's earnings, and the amount required to complete the works. Mentioning that the 'lower mile and a half from Mr. Raby's Ironworks to the sea' had been opened in May 1803, he reported that the tolls received in 1803 amounted to £125, and in 1804 to £425. He continued:

> This year they are expected considerably to increase: the Ironstone likely to be brought down to the Furnaces this year, from the upper part of the Road, will produce about £600, which in subsequent years will be greatly augmented as the Mine works upon the Mountain are more opened. There are stone-coal [anthracite] and culm collieries along the whole line of the Road which from the parties working them there is reason for considerable expectations; but as these collieries have been hitherto only opened for country sale, it takes a length of time to extend them so as to produce a sufficient quantity to spare for shipping.

After these obviously encouraging observations, Shewen concluded by setting out accounts which showed that although £26,643 had already been spent, £5,500 was required from subscribers in order to balance the books.

	Dr.	£		Cr.	£
To	Original Shares	18,500	By expenditure Compleating Rail Road to Mountain Including Balances due to Sundry Persons		26,643
	New Shares	6,500			
	Amt. reqd. to finish	5,500	Calculation for Finishing the Road to the Lime Rock		2,234
			Ditto the Dock		1,623
		30,500			30,500

Business at the Llanelly end of the line developed rapidly assisted by the exceptional stimulus of the Napoleonic Wars. In November 1805, James Barnes presented plans and estimates for further improvements to the dock, and in the same month the company noted that parts of the tramroad needed repair. Already numerous short branches had been built to serve nearby works, most of which were under Raby's direction; now it was decided to ease congestion by doubling the tramroad 'from the Turnout Place at the Lime Kiln' (Cwmddyche) down to 'the Turnout place at Old Castle'. To avoid delay it was proposed to do this by 'taking up the Upper Mine Road and putting down the rails to make the Rail Road double from the Furnace to the Dock'. A decision in favour of this move was taken at Llanelly on 16th November, 1805, but a week later it was queried by London shareholders, who had provided much of the capital and who now had formed their own committee.

The eventual outcome of this proposal is not clear, but what is apparent is that the London shareholders felt that they were not being kept fully in-

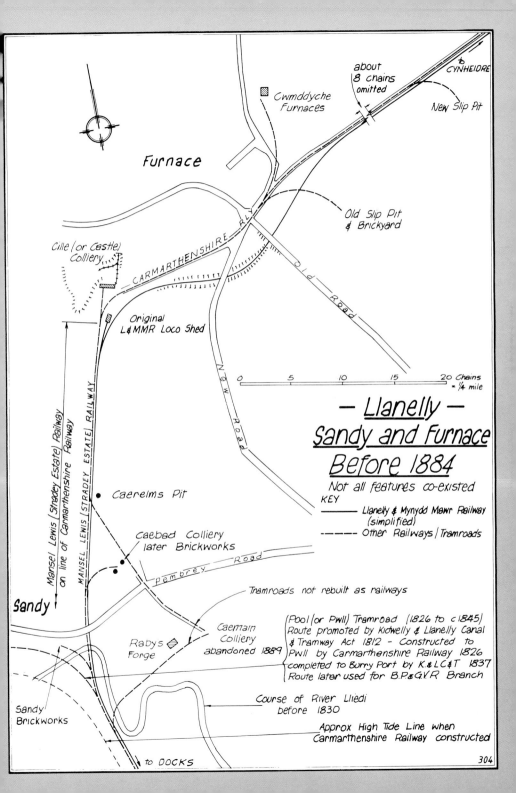

to
CYNHEIDRE

about
8 chains
omitted

New Slip Pit

Cwmddyche
Furnaces

Furnace

Old Slip Pit
& Brickyard

Cille (or Castle)
Colliery

CARMARTHENSHIRE RLY

Old Road

Original
L&MMR Loco Shed

New Road

0   5   10   15   20 Chains
= ¼ mile

— Llanelly —
Sandy and Furnace
Before 1884

Not all features co-existed

KEY

——— Llanelly & Mynydd Mawr Railway
(simplified)
------- Other Railways/Tramroads

Mansel Lewis (Stradey Estate) Railway
on line of Carmarthenshire Railway

MANSEL LEWIS (STRADEY ESTATE) RAILWAY

Caerelms Pit

Caebad Colliery
later Brickworks

Pembrey Road

Tramroads not rebuilt as railways

Sandy

Caemain
Colliery
abandoned 1889

Rabys
Forge

(Pool (or Pwll) Tramroad (1826 to c1845)
Route promoted by Kidwelly & Llanelly Canal
& Tramway Act 1812 - Constructed to
Pwll by Carmarthenshire Railway 1826
completed to Burry Port by K.&LC&T 1837
Route later used for B.P.&G.V.R Branch

Course of River Lliedi
before 1830

Sandy
Brickworks

Approx High Tide Line when
Carmarthenshire Railway constructed

to DOCKS

304

formed. Indeed they were becoming increasingly concerned about the company's management. Doubling track and dock improvements (which in 1806 included a weir and a reservoir) might imply growing commercial success, but in reality profits were lacking and trouble was brewing for Alexander Raby. For this he was at least partly to blame, because almost from the outset he seems to have misused the company's money. Under the 1802 Act a General Assembly (or shareholder's meeting) could be held if proprietors controlling a majority of the shares (that is to say, at least 126) were present, or represented by proxy. By July 1805, Raby held 42 shares and proxies for another 96. Taking advantage of his dominant position, he seems to have run the railway as though he were the sole owner. He expended company capital on additional branch lines and sidings to serve his own industrial sites, and to make matters worse he appears to have evaded paying tolls for his own use of the tramroad. As a major user of the line, his behaviour had a serious effect on the company's income, inhibiting the payment of dividends. Little wonder he faced increasing suspicion!

Alexander Raby effectively exploited his distance from the London shareholders, and it might be said that he showed considerable entrepreneurial enterprise in doing so. However the London shareholders could not be fooled for long, and at a General Assembly held on 7th November, 1805, it was agreed that both Llanelly and London interests should be represented on the proprietors' committee. The London Committee was set up, and pressed for a full investigation of Alexander Raby's accounts, which were said to be 'of such magnitude and importance as it is feared involves . . . the ruin or recovery of the company's affairs' (see Appendix 1). The issue came to a head on 15th August, 1806, when a report was presented to a specially convened General Assembly, following an enquiry and survey carried out by James Barnes and three others. The criticism of Raby was damning. It emerged that he had built almost five miles of unauthorised branches, and whilst some had been well used, others had hardly been worked at all. Their existence was said to be 'unsufferable'. It was noted that in the vicinity of the ironworks Mr Raby 'travails upon these branches without coming upon the weighing machine', and the report proposed the erection of two more weighing machines. It was also noted that 'Mr Raby lands his Lancashire ore on the beach within the Parliamentary limits and thus evades the dock dues; not only so, but the carts which bring it to his depot go upon and over the road and do considerable damage thereto'. The railway was certainly suffering as well. In July 1807, Rhys Davies described it as being in a 'bad plight as you will see by the advertisements renting the tolls and the right of finishing the last mile and three-quarters for which the Railroad company has no money.'

Unfortunately, Raby's side of the story is not recorded, but his obvious reluctance to pay tolls and dock dues may mean that he had serious financial worries long before this report was produced. There seems little doubt that his collieries were often difficult to work, and less successful than he anticipated, to the extent that it may have been difficult to meet the somewhat onerous terms in his leases. The importation of iron ore from Lancashire indicates that Raby had been badly advised about the local ore, which seems to have been relatively low in iron. But whatever may be said in Raby's defence, there is no doubt that he misused the funds of the Carmarthenshire Railway and over-reached himself financially. Arguably he was over-trading, that is to say spending more than profits in the hope of generating expansion. If so, he gambled heavily and he lost, in spite of the industrial prosperity created by the Napoleonic Wars.

In June 1807, facing the possibility of bankruptcy proceedings, Raby surrendered his estates to his creditors to be sold to reduce his debts. Accordingly he parted with two properties in London, two estates in Worcestershire, and land in Surrey. He also handed over the leases of his coal, copper and iron interests to trustees who were empowered to sell them if matters got worse. In return he was allowed to keep control of his industrial activities, so that he might have some chance of making a recovery.

After such a crisis, recovery was never likely to be easy. In September 1807, Raby's trustees received a notice of ejection from the Stradey estate; Raby replied that coal production had been low because seams in the Shipping Colliery had been thinner than their description in the 1798 lease. More positively, though, Raby developed the Box Colliery at Llanelly, much encouraged by finding a coal seam nine feet thick. Although he was raising coal at Box in November 1808, and moving it to the dock over a branch of the Carmarthenshire Railway, it was really too little and too late. The proceeds of the sale of his estates had proved to be inadequate to satisfy his creditors, and his trustees were obliged to auction his other industrial and leasehold interests. This sale took place at Garraway's Coffee House, Cornhill, in the City of London on 16th November, 1809. All Raby's interests at Llanelly were included in the sale, being listed as the Box Colliery, the Stradey Estate collieries, two iron furnaces, a 'newly erected Forge and Rolling Mill', workmens' and managers' houses, iron railways, steam engines and certain farm leases. Raby's heyday at Llanelly was now over. He was close to bankruptcy once more, and was rescued only by loans from the proprietors of the Llanelly Copperworks Company, Charles and Richard Janion Nevill. Their influence in the affairs of the Carmarthenshire Railway, and of Llanelly itself, grew as Raby's influence declined.

The old mill at Furnace, with Raby's furnace on the extreme left of the photograph.
Llanelli Public Library

Chapter Three
The Carmarthenshire Railway in decline

In these early years the fortunes of the Carmarthenshire Railway fluctuated with the fortunes (or misfortunes) of Alexander Raby. Following the financial crisis of November 1809, it appears that for a time the railway was almost at a standstill. The word 'almost' is used advisedly, because it is not clear to what extent Raby's coal and iron making activities were able to function in 1810. New investment at this period seems to have been concentrated on the promising Caemain colliery, but at a time when Raby's greatest need was for an income, and the Nevills must have been looking for some return on their loans, it seems improbable that everything else would have been allowed to stagnate. At any rate by 1811 Raby was in business and the situation seems to have been improving. Indeed, in April 1811, a new 416 yd-long branch engineered by Henry David and David Hugh was opened, linking the Carmarthenshire Railway with General Warde's pits at Erwfawr, east of Old Castle. It did not have a long life, and was probably closed by 1817.

Charles Nevill died in 1813, but Richard, his son, continued to give Raby his backing. In doing so, he was not disinterested. Perhaps anticipating further financial setbacks, R.J. Nevill took over more and more of Raby's assets whilst at the same time doing his utmost to avoid his debts. In January 1816, overall control of the Stradey Estate collieries was transferred to Trustees acting for Raby's creditors, Raby and his son Arthur being permitted to retain some powers of management at the not ungenerous salaries of £500 and £200 respectively. Thereafter, although there was some investment in the Caemain colliery, very little was applied to the railway or other works.

It is very probable that by 1816 traffic on the Carmarthenshire Railway north of Cynheidre had ceased, although any suggestion that the remainder was also moribund is much less likely. In 1814 a direct link was built between Box Colliery and R.J. Nevill's Wern line through Llanelly which effectively diverted Box traffic away from the Carmarthenshire's branch to the colliery. In the following year, even before the depression had set in after the Napoleonic Wars, the furnace at Cwmddyche was blown out. Traffic on the railway must have slumped, but it is by no means certain that it halted. Not only were there small collieries at work near the railway in Llanelly, but the Brondini Colliery at Cynheidre appears to have been active until 1827, and it is unlikely that coal would have been moved away other than by tramroad. Furthermore, in 1826 a branch of 1½ miles was opened linking the Pwll colliery with Sandy and Llanelly. Constructed at a cost of £2,770 by the Kidwelly & Llanelly Canal & Tramroad Co. (K&LCT), the line was largely financed by the Carmarthenshire Railway which took shares in the K&LCT. R.J. Nevill also purchased shares, and negotiated for the lease of New Lodge Colliery, west of Pwll, which was already linked by tramroad to the new harbour further to the west known as Pembrey.

Reference to the Kidwelly & Llanelly Canal, and to Pembrey, make it appropriate to make brief mention of transport developments in the Gwendraeth Valley. As early as 1769 a wealthy Pembrokeshire man, Thomas

Kymer, had completed a canal from his coal pits and quarries at Pwllylly-
goed, near Carway, to a new quay at Kidwelly, a distance of 3½ miles. In
1793 it was suggested that this canal be extended further inland, but no
action was taken. In 1811, however, a scheme was prepared not only to
extend the canal to Pontyberem, but also to construct a canal branch to
Llanelly. The prospectus for the Kidwelly & Llanelly Canal Company was
issued in October 1811, and had the support of some powerful local land-
owners, including Lord Ashburnham, Lord Cawdor and Lord Dynevor.
Although the prospectus anticipated the export of 200 tons of coal per day at
Kidwelly and 100 tons per day at Llanelly, in Llanelly the project was
perceived as a threat because it was thought likely to divert traffic towards
Kidwelly over the contemplated canal connection. On 29th October, 1811,
the Carmarthenshire Railway held a Special General Assembly at which it
was resolved to petition Parliament regarding any application by others to
unite with the railway or dock, or to interfere with the Company's powers
granted under their Act of 1802. However, the Kidwelly & Llanelly Canal
and Tramroad Company obtained its Act in 1812, and it included authority
not only to improve and extend Kymer's Canal by canal or tramroad to
Cwm-y-Glo, near Cwmmawr, but also to build a canal or tramroad branch
from Spudders Bridge to a basin at Old Castle House, Llanelly. In fact the
main line of the canal was extended inland as far as Pontyates, to join a
tramroad feeder from the north-west. The branch canal was only built to
Pen-y-bedd, near Pembrey, and not extended to Pembrey New Harbour
(otherwise known as Burry Port) until 1837. It was only then, when a
tramroad connection to Llanelly was also provided, that the fears of Llanelly
people proved to be justified.

The prospect of the harbour at Kidwelly developing at the expense of
Llanelly, together with the effects of an immense storm in October 1812,
which caused serious damage to the small docks along the coast, may have
been a factor in the promotion of another Parliamentary Bill to establish the
Burry Harbour Commissioners. However, the principal reason was undoubtedly to improve conditions in the notoriously dangerous Burry Estuary. By an Act of 1813 no less than 59 people were appointed Commissioners and given powers to improve and regulate navigation on the Rivers
Burry, Loughor and Lliedi. They were also empowered to levy dues on ships
crossing the bar at the entrance to the rivers in order to meet the costs arising
in their area of responsibility – which extended as far as Llangennech on the
River Loughor and to the Iron Bridge at Sandy on the River Lliedi. It appears
that one of their first achievements was a harbour improvement scheme at
Llanelly which included the construction of a long breakwater from the
western arm of the Carmarthenshire Dock, thereby giving vessels greater
protection from heavy seas.

By February 1821, Raby's rent arrears were such that the then owner of the
Stradey estate, Thomas Lewis, had machinery and plant at Caemain valued
under a distress order. Once again R.J. Nevill provided money to pay the
most pressing creditors, but now he took over exclusive control and management of Raby's properties. Under his direction the Rabys were allowed to
continue coal mining, but output fell so much that by Lady Day, 1823, they

were unable to pay royalties due to Thomas Lewis. By the end of the year their debts amounted to £13,000 and Alexander was obliged to transfer his interests in Llanelly to Arthur. Accordingly Arthur worked coal under leases formerly held by his father, and in 1824 even developed a pit at Kille (or Cille) Farm. Early in the summer of 1826, however, R.J. Nevill assumed complete control, and Alexander Raby left Llanelly after 30 years, minus his fortune. He died at Wells, Somerset early in 1835, aged 88 or 89.

Thomas Lewis, owner of the Stradey estate, died in 1829, and was succeeded by his son, David Lewis. The historian Robin Craig, who has made a diligent study of the Mansel Lewis papers, has noted that at some date before 1832 the Stradey estate built its own line from Cwmddyche and Cille to the Carmarthenshire Dock. The track was laid parallel to, and to the west of the Carmarthenshire Railway, and made a junction with Nevill's private line opposite the 'Hope & Anchor' hostelry close to the Carmarthenshire Dock, and also a junction with the new branch from Pwll colliery. As Lewis did not provide any motive power or rolling stock of his own, he made working agreements with R.J. Nevill which effectively enabled Nevill to reach the outposts of his expanding empire on the west side of Llanelly.

As the Lewis family had shares in the Carmarthenshire Railway, and might be expected to wish it well, the building of this line is curious. Assuming the construction was not motivated by a desire to avoid Carmarthenshire tolls, it must be supposed that the Stradey estate line was an edge railway and not a plateway, like the Carmarthenshire line. There may also have been a difference in gauge. In the 1820s the tide of expert opinion swung strongly in favour of edge railways, which could handle much heavier loads. At this period the Carmarthenshire Railway may well have appeared less than adequate for increasing traffic to and from the Stradey estate. If so, it must be supposed that even in Llanelly the Carmarthenshire's plateway track was probably out of use before 1832. According to a map accompanying the 1835 prospectus of the Llanelly Railway & Dock Co., the Carmarthenshire line was then 'broken up' about a mile north of Felin Foel (that is to say beyond Quarry Mawr).

The unhappy state of the Carmarthenshire Railway, and the perceived advantages of edge railways, gave rise to a scheme in 1833 to rebuild the horse drawn tramroad. On 27th June, 1834, the Carmarthenshire Railway obtained an Act giving powers to relay their line as an edge railway, and to operate locomotives. For this purpose the Act also authorized an additional share capital of £12,000 and loans amounting to £6,000. The project became the subject of some debate, but on 22nd December, 1835, there was a meeting at Llanelly at which one William Brunton submitted an estimate of £9,452 for relaying the railway. Several colliery proprietors, including David Lewis and Messrs Greatrex & Sayce, offered their support, but the work was not put in hand.

The reason may well have been linked with the fact that in 1835 the Llanelly Railway obtained powers to build a 4 ft 8½ in. gauge edge railway from the foot of their incline on the St David's (Dafen) branch to connect with the Carmarthenshire Railway at Felin Foel. It was anticipated then that the Carmarthenshire Railway would be altered to edge rails in accordance

with its 1834 Act. By the Llanelly Railway's 1835 Act, however, that company also obtained powers to build a standard gauge line from Llanelly to
Llandilo, with several branches. One of these was to run from Dyffryn Lodge
(Tirydail) to a terminus at Gorsgoch Colliery, near Cross Hands, on Mynydd
Mawr. By this means the Llanelly Railway sought access to the mineral
wealth of Mynydd Mawr at a moment when Llanelly's industry was expanding rapidly.

The approach to Mynydd Mawr by this route involved the provision of an
immense rope-worked incline, well over 600 yards long. Although work on
most of the railways authorised by the 1835 Act began energetically in the
spring of 1836, the direct connection with the Carmarthenshire at Felin Foel
was not made. On 1st June, 1840, the annual meeting of the proprietors of
the Llanelly Railway heard that the line to Cwm Amman (Garnant) was
open, and that the 1½ miles of main line from Parkrhyn (Pantyffynon) to
Duffryn Lodge was 'nearly completed'. The report continued:

> The branch leading to Mr Long Wrey's Collieries and Messrs Morris Sayce & Co's is
> in course of forward progress, and will be completed by 1 January next. This
> branch is altogether about 4 miles in length, and leads to several collieries of
> capital. The company have entered into a contract with Mr Wrey to bring for seven
> years at least 10,000 tons yearly down this branch, which will yield Railway &
> Dock dues as a minimum amount the sum of £1,000 p.a.

It appears that public traffic to Duffryn Lodge actually began on 6th May,
1841, and that mineral traffic on the Mountain branch officially began on the
same day.

Meanwhile, on the west side of Llanelly, the Kidwelly & Llanelly Canal
Co. had been active also, and was taking an interest in Carmarthenshire
Railway territory. In 1833 the K & LCT asked their Engineer, James Green, to
inspect the canal, and also all unfinished works, and to provide estimates for
their completion. Subsequently he was asked to survey the route for the
intended canal up the Gwendraeth valley from Pontyates to Cwm-y-Glo,
near Cross Hands. In his report he advocated that the canal be built as far as
Cwm Mawr, utilising three inclined planes, but declared that beyond that
point the rise was too rapid to warrant the extension of the canal. He
continued:

> The Coal property above Cwm Mawr will have a ready and convenient access to
> the Canal at that place . . . and as the Company have the power to lay down a
> branch Railroad from Cwm Mawr in the direction of Blaenhirwain, which branch
> may be made to connect itself . . . with the upper part of the Carmarthenshire
> Railway, near the Tumble Colliery, all the Coal district with which the upper part
> of the Carmarthenshire Railway communicates, will find its way to the head of
> your Canal, and thence to the new Harbour at Pembrey.

Although James Green believed that initially the River Gwendraeth would
provide enough water for the canal at Cwm Mawr, he foresaw such an
increase in traffic as to necessitate an additional reservoir. Referring to his
latest estimates of expense, he described the cost of a reservoir above Cwm-
y-glo bridge as 'trivial', even though it was to cover 59 acres. He added,
'though . . . it may not for some years be required, I cannot hesitate to

recommend its formation, as it must put the supply of Water to the Canal beyond question.'

Much of the work proposed by this report of October 1833, was carried out. The canal was extended up the valley to Cwm Mawr, although there is doubt whether the uppermost of the three inclined planes was ever completed. Instead it is thought that a tramroad over this section sufficed for the traffic. It is also thought that a tramroad was constructed up the hill from Cwm Mawr towards Tumble and the Carmarthenshire Railway, but it is not known how far this extended. What is clear is that a reservoir was built at Cwm-y-glo, although it may never have been filled to its capacity. There is also good evidence of a branch tramroad from the formation of the Carmarthenshire Railway at Cross Hands towards the reservoir dam. This fact makes it quite possible to speculate that the canal company followed James Green's recommendations, and simply leased or 'adopted' part of the Carmarthenshire line in order to reach Cwm-y-glo. Unfortunately the truth of what actually happened has yet to emerge; it is not certain that coal traffic from Cross Hands was ever taken down to the Kidwelly & Llanelly Canal with any regularity. The same report made mention of the cost of extending the tramway from New Lodge to Pwll, west of Llanelly.

Early in July 1837, the Kidwelly & Llanelly Canal & Tramroad Company completed its line from Pembrey to Llanelly. It celebrated the occasion by moving two 'cargoes' of coal from Pwll colliery west to Burry Port for shipment. *The Cambrian* reported on 8th July that,

> The waggons came down in procession, with colours flying, and on their arrival at the dock, where the vessels were all decorated, were received with hearty cheers, firing of guns etc., by a crowd of persons collected on the occasion. This railway, and the canal up the Gwendraeth, have been completed to communicate with the new floating dock at Pembrey, called Burry Port, which is unquestionably the best shipping place in South Wales, having at the lowest neap tides 13 feet of water through the dock gates, and 24 feet at spring tides.

Plainly what was good news for Burry Port was not such good news for Llanelly, but such was the rate of Llanelly's growth that the development seems to have caused rather less concern in 1837 than the threat of it had done in 1811 and 1812. In fact in 1837 David Lewis, assisted by the mining engineer R.W. Jones, began work on a coal pit and level at Cwmddyche, close to Raby's abandoned furnace. This came into production in 1838, and by 1840 was producing 100 tons of saleable coal per week. In that year, for the first time, coal from Cwmddyche was sent via the new tramroad for export from Burry Port rather than Llanelly. Although the rail journey was longer, the barque *Amazon* appears to have been loaded promptly. If Raby had still been alive he would also have been concerned to learn that in September 1839, for the first time, anthracite coal from Mynydd Mawr was transported over the Llanelly Railway to the New Docks, Llanelly, for the export overseas.

The difficulties of shipping from Llanelly – primarily the problem of harbour silting – were becoming so serious at a period when ever larger ships were being built that the Harbour Commissioners felt obliged to seek further powers to deal with the matter. By an Act of 1843 they were authorised to borrow another £20,000, to make and maintain protective sea walls, and also to build a scouring reservoir on the site of what later became the North Dock. More significantly for this history, they were also empowered to purchase the Carmarthenshire Dock, and given this authority the Commissioners soon opened negotiations with the Carmarthenshire Railway. At a meeting of the company held at Llanelly on 18th May, 1844, the proprietors resolved to dispose of both the dock and the railway, and David Lewis and R.J. Nevill were authorised to negotiate the transaction. Unfortunately the exact terms of the arrangements made are now obscure, but the transfer of the dock appears to have facilitated the completion of the 'new cut', shortening the course of the River Lliedi by diverting it to run through the north end of the Carmarthenshire Dock and into the sea. Although, after many years of struggle, the Carmarthenshire Railway had ceased trading in or before 1844, the company itself was not dissolved and evidently retained ownership of the line.

As these matters were being decided in Llanelly, a Bill was being presented to Parliament for the construction of the South Wales Railway (SWR), running from Gloucester to the Pembrokeshire coast near Fishguard. Engineered on the broad gauge by the famous I.K. Brunel, the SWR was an offshoot of the Great Western Railway, and was very soon leased by it. The SWR was incorporated in 1845, and by an Act of 1846 certain alterations of alignment were permitted, including a slight amendment to the route of the railway along the coast between Llanelly and Pembrey. As this section was across foreshore in the ownership of the Crown, the 1845 Act contained the interesting and slightly surprising provision that this part of the SWR should be built under the supervision of H.M. Commissioners of Woods and Forests.

The result of building the SWR's long railway embankment across the foreshore, together with the diversion of the River Lliedi at Llanelly, was to exclude the sea from a large area extending from Old Castle in the east to Pwll in the west, effectively closing Pwll Quay. When questions were asked about the ownership of the newly drained land, the Crown entered into discussions with David Lewis of Stradey. In what John Innes, the Llanelly historian, described as an 'astonishing and unfortunate compromise' the Crown granted Lewis all its interest in the land and minerals between the railway bridge over the new cut at Old Castle, the South Wales Railway, and the west side of the Stradey (or Yard) River near Pwll. Even more surprisingly, Lewis was also given title to land (but not minerals) on the seaward side of the SWR down to the low water mark. The effect of this arrangement was to provide a very sizeable extension to the Stradey estate.

The Lewis private railway, which now had a complete monopoly over the traffic from the Stradey estate to the Carmarthenshire Dock, was one of several existing lines in the Llanelly area to be provided with a flat crossing over the SWR. Meanwhile the Mynydd Mawr area was also being served by the Mountain branch of the Llanelly Railway, and the partially dismantled Carmarthenshire Railway was little more than a footpath from Llanelly inland to Mynydd Mawr. The SWR from Landore (Swansea) to Carmarthen was eventually opened on 11th October, 1852. The influential David Lewis of Stradey rode from Swansea to Pembrey on the locomotive with Isambard Kingdom Brunel.

Chapter Four
The Dormant Tramroad

As the abandoned Carmarthenshire Railway lay cold and quiet, a number of local undertakings sought, by one means or another, to pick over the bones of the old company. In Llanelly, the Harbour Commissioners went to Parliament in 1858 for powers to carry out certain improvements, including the reconstruction of the Carmarthenshire Dock as a floating dock, and the provision of a scouring reservoir. The floating dock was never built, although sluice gates and the necessary embankments for the reservoir at the head of the dock were constructed. The same Act authorised the building of two railways, the first of which ran from the SWR west of the River Lliedi, south to the end of the western harbour breakwater. This line appears to have taken the alignment of the Carmarthenshire Railway on the west side of the Carmarthenshire Dock, although it terminated further south, as the breakwater was then being extended by the dumping of slag. This railway was built, apparently to the 7 ft 0¼ in. broad gauge of the SWR. The second railway authorised was not constructed. It had been intended to run from the junction with the SWR already described on a line to the south of, and parallel with, the SWR to an end-on junction with the Llanelly Railway just east of the SWR's Llanelly station. The fact that the Llanelly Railway was built to the standard gauge of 4 ft 8½ in. was probably the main reason that this second railway was not built.

As early as 1853 the ambitious Carmarthen and Cardigan Railway (C&CR) had plans not only to link the two towns named in its title, but also to extend eastwards across the head of the Gwendraeth Valley to meet the Llanelly Railway's Mountain branch at Gorsgoch. This line, the C&CR's Cross Hands branch, was intended to tap anthracite traffic from collieries near the northern end of the Carmarthenshire Railway. It was included in the C&CR's proposals primarily to satisfy one of that company's chief supporters, Edward Fitzwilliams, who wanted to obtain a reliable supply of coal for his lime kilns at Van, north of Kidwelly. By the end of 1853, however, this branch scheme had to be dropped for want of finance, and Fitzwilliams was deeply displeased. Faced with financial problems of his own he later left both the C&CR Board and the country.

In spite of his departure, the C&CR, whose plans were almost always a triumph of aspiration over realism, entertained dreams of extending into the Gwendraeth Valley. In the autumn of 1861 the company promoted a Bill which not only sought powers to extend their main line, but also included provisions to build branches from Kidwelly to Mynydd-y-Garreg, and also to Carway, Pontyberem and the Carmarthenshire Railway near Cwm Blawd. Noting this, *The Cambrian* newspaper reported approvingly in December 1861, that 'for some time past the propriety of opening up the Gwendraeth by a mineral line has been discussed, and the Carmarthenshire tramroad still being in tolerable preservation steps were taken for its restoration, which could easily be accomplished . . .' In the event, by the time the Bill was passed, all the provisions for branches from Kidwelly had gone, and the Act referred only to the C&CR's broad gauge main line north from Carmarthen.

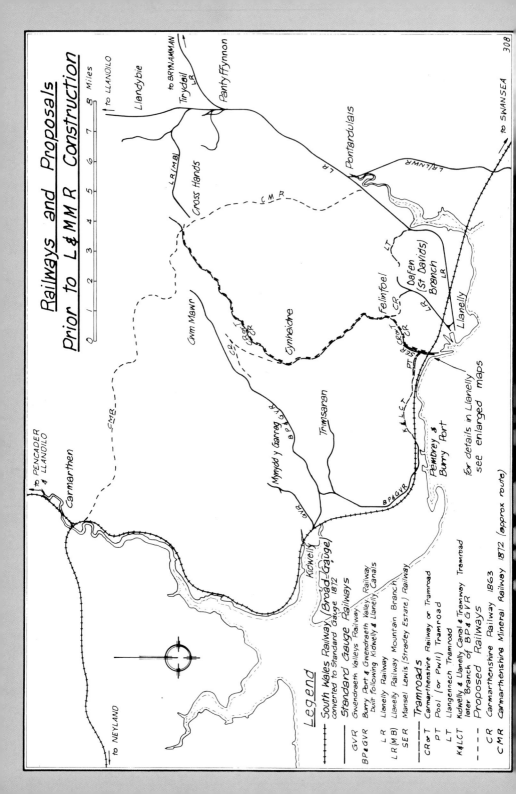

Railways and Proposals
Prior to L & M M R Construction

0 1 2 3 4 5 6 7 8 Miles

to NEYLAND

to PENCADER & LLANDILO

Carmarthen

to LLANDILO

Llandybie

to BRYNAMMAN

Tirydail

Pantyffynnon

Cross Hands

Pontarddulais

to SWANSEA

Cwm Mawr

Cynheidre

Felinfoel

Dafen (St Davids) Branch

Llanelly

Trimsaran

Mynydd y Garreg

Pembrey & Burry Port

Kidwelly

for details in Llanelly
see enlarged maps

Legend

━━━━ South Wales Railway (Broad-Gauge)
converted to Standard Gauge 1872

Standard Gauge Railways

GVR   Gwendraeth Valleys Railway
BP & GVR   Burry Port & Gwendraeth Valley Railway
           built following Kidwelly & Llanelly Canals
LR   Llanelly Railway
LR (MB)   Llanelly Railway Mountain Branch
SER   Mansel Lewis (Stradey Estate) Railway

Tramroads

CR or T   Carmarthenshire Railway or Tramroad
PT   Pool (or Pwll) Tramroad
LT   Llangennech Tramroad
K & LCT   Kidwelly & Llanelly Canal & Tramway Tramroad
           later Branch of BP & GVR

Proposed Railways

- - - -   Carmarthenshire Railway 1863
CR
CMR   Carmarthenshire Mineral Railway 1872 (approx route)

308

Even this work proved to be difficult: by 1864 the company had only completed the 18 miles from Carmarthen to Llandyssul. There the C&CR remained, although in 1864 the company did obtain powers to build an entirely separate line from Kidwelly to Velindre, near Mynydd-y-Garreg, primarily for limestone traffic. It is believed that some construction work took place, but eventually this final manifestation of the C&CR's Gwendraeth Valley dreams was built by an entirely distinct company spawned by the C&CR. Appropriately entitled the Gwendraeth Valleys Railway, it opened for mineral and freight traffic in 1871.

The Carmarthenshire Railway's close neighbour, the Llanelly Railway, was another concern with designs on the old tramroad route. As early as 1845 the Llanelly Railway may have been influential in the promotion of the Carmarthenshire Mineral Junction Railway. This was intended to create a direct link over 12 miles long between Carmarthen and the terminus of the Mountain branch, crossing the Carmarthenshire Railway near Cross Hands. It did not proceed, and was merely the precursor of the abortive Carmarthen and Cardigan scheme of 1853.

The year 1863 witnessed a more determined attempt to rebuild the old tramroad. In that year the Llanelly Railway was involved in the promotion of a Parliamentary Bill in the name of the Carmarthenshire Railway. The intention now was to reconstruct the old line to modern standards on the 4 ft 8½ in. gauge, to provide a connection to the Llanelly Railway's St David's branch (Dafen) from Felin Foel, and a branch from Cynheidre to Coalbrook (Pontyberem) and Carway. The effect of the link to the St David's branch would have been to create a through route from Cross Hands via Dafen into the Llanelly Railway's docks, avoiding the incline on the Mountain branch. The effect of the new lines to Coalbrook (Pontyberem) and Carway was to give the Llanelly Railway access to the territory and traffic of the Kidwelly & Llanelly Canal Co., and their unfinished extension towards Cwmmawr.

Surveyed by the engineers C.B. Lane and Edward Bagot, the new Carmarthenshire company was authorised by Act of Parliament in 1864 with a capital of £125,000 in £10 shares and borrowing powers of up to £41,000. A year later another Act was passed permitting the compulsory purchase of additional land, and the transfer of a portion of the proposed line (the connection to St David's) to the Llanelly Railway. The Carmarthenshire's share capital was now reduced by £15,000, and its borrowing powers by £5,000. By 1866 (if not earlier) the Secretary of the new company was Richard Glascodine, who held the office of Superintendent and Secretary on the Llanelly Railway.

The Llanelly Railway's interest in the Carmarthenshire concern is also evident in surviving correspondence between the company and David Lewis of Stradey. It would appear that Lewis was being encouraged to finance the building of the line between Old Castle and Furnace for the benefit of the Stradey estate. In November 1865, a Mr Douglas estimated that a single line of railway 114 chains long, from Pentrepoeth Cottages at Furnace to the South Wales Railway would cost £5,500. He added that a short branch to Caemain would cost £530, and a 55 chain connection from Furnace to the junction at Felin Foel with the proposed link to St David's would cost £1,870.

Initially the matter was allowed to rest, although it seems that in 1866 a siding was built from SWR to Old Castle to serve the Old Castle Tinplate works then under construction. In August 1867, J.W. Cole of the Llanelly Railway's Engineers Department provided David Lewis with a new estimate. He considered that the proposed line from the Old Castle Tinplate works to Furnace would require 1,980 yds of rails weighing 100 tons, and he calculated the cost of 220 yds of track to Old Castle colliery, and a further 418 yds of track between the tinplate works and the SWR. Relaying the track from Old Castle to Furnace on the standard gauge was carried out, but only two months later the Llanelly Railway had second thoughts about its involvement. On 15th October, 1867, Richard Glascodine wrote to David Lewis to say that the 'promoters of the scheme for relaying (the Carmarthenshire Railway) . . . came to the conclusion it would not be expedient to relay the upper portion unless the outlet to the Port were also to be the property of and under the control of the proposed company. So far as their enquiries have led hitherto they find that the absence of an arrangement on this point is a great obstacle to their obtaining promises of money to carry out the project.' Accordingly Glascodine asked if Lewis would be willing to surrender any rights he might have over the lower portion of the line 'including that which you have relaid at your own cost, so that the old Tramroad may be fully in the possession of the company proposed to be formed.' It must be assumed that these discussions were difficult, because the Llanelly Railway did not proceed. Apart from David Lewis' use of part of the tramroad for the Stradey estate's edge railway, the Carmarthenshire Railway scheme of the 1860s failed to materialise.

Nevertheless, the project had repercussions, both in the Gwendraeth Valley and in Llanelly. In 1864 it was certainly seen as a considerable threat to the livelihood of the Kidwelly & Llanelly Canal Co. Thoroughly alarmed, this concern went to Parliament for powers to convert its canal into a railway. When its Bill became an Act on 5th July, 1865, the undertaking became known as the Kidwelly & Burry Port Railway. A year later it was renamed again, to become the Burry Port & Gwendraeth Valley Railway (BP & GVR). Rebuilding ensued, and the new railway was opened for mineral traffic between Burry Port and Pontyberem in July 1869. A branch to Kidwelly was opened in June 1873, (with a connection to the Gwendraeth Valleys Railway), but the extension to Cwmmawr was not completed until June 1886. After the BP & GVR took over traffic working on the Gwendraeth Valleys Railway in 1874 it became the true inheritor of all the assorted proposals to build railways up the Gwendraeth Valley.

Although the 1864 Carmarthenshire Railway scheme failed, the Llanelly Railway (LR) itself continued to make progress. For a better understanding of later events it is appropriate to give a brief account of the LR's development. By 1868 it had expanded to comprise not only the main line north to Llandilo (with the branches mentioned earlier), but also an extension to Llandovery (The Vale of Towy Railway, opened 1858), and branches from Llandilo to Carmarthen (1864), Pontardulais to Swansea Victoria (1866) and Gowerton – Penclawdd (1867). Unfortunately, the company's advance was then checked when it was persuaded to share responsibility for working the

Vale of Towy line with the powerful London & North Western Railway, which controlled the Central Wales Railway to the north.

Under the provisions of the joint lease the Llanelly Railway conceded running powers to the LNWR from Llandovery south to Carmarthen, Llanelly and Swansea. This was a serious error, and although the LR soon realised its mistake, it was unable to rectify the matter in the courts. Under an Act of 1871 the Llanelly Railway was effectively split in two, the Llandilo–Carmarthen and Pontardulais–Swansea lines being formed into a separate company, which was bought out by the LNWR only two years later. Although the Vale of Towy continued to be jointly worked, the much reduced Llanelly Railway of just 36 miles was not strong enough to maintain its independence for long. The Great Western Railway, which had taken over the South Wales Railway in 1863 now leased the LR with effect from 1st January, 1873. In May 1872 the GWR had abolished the broad gauge in South Wales, and had thereby removed the chief difference between its system and local standard gauge concerns like the LR. The GWR eventually absorbed the Llanelly Railway & Dock Co. completely in 1889.

The elimination of Brunel's broad gauge probably contributed to fresh thoughts about the reconstruction of the Carmarthenshire Railway or Tramroad. In 1872 an Act was passed authorising the building of the Carmarthenshire Mineral Railway. Surveyed by J. Brunton and R.J. George this line was intended to run from Carmarthen to Ponthendy, south of Pontardulais, with a branch from Llandarrog to Ffan (or Van). At Cross Hands there was to be a spur to the Mountain branch, and another to the Carmarthenshire Tramroad, which was to be rebuilt to a point as far south as Cwmblawd. This project, like so many others, did not proceed, but in the following year a Mr George (possibly the R.J. George mentioned) was associated with a proposal to reconstruct 'the old Carmarthenshire Railway' as a standard gauge line by forming a new company with a capital of £90,000 in 9,000 £10 shares. This idea was felt to be particularly attractive to colliery proprietors on Mynydd Mawr, who encountered irritating delays in sending their coal down the massive incline on the Mountain branch.

By November 1874, a Committee appointed to look into all aspects of the proposal had prepared a report. The Committee members (C.W. Nevill, William Rosser, William Thomas, Henry Rees and Joshua Buckley) took the view that Parliamentary powers should be sought to form a new company, and they noted that the necessary plans and notices had been prepared already by an experienced railway engineer, Mr W.R. Kinipple. Somewhat surprisingly, his estimate of the cost of the work, the provisions of stock and other contingencies came to just £45,000. This low figure had the merit of halving the deposit of 5 per cent of the estimated value of the works which was payable to the Court of Chancery before proceeding with the Bill.

The early promises of support must have been encouraging, because the Act was duly applied for in 1875. In accordance with Parliamentary Standing Orders, on 31st May, 1875, a Special General Assembly of the proprietors of the Carmarthenshire Railway was held at the Town Hall, Llanelly to discuss the 'Bill being promoted in the present session of Parliament intitled [sic] "A Bill for authorizing the construction of a Railway from

Llanelly to Mynydd Mawr in the County of Carmarthen; for conferring powers on the Carmarthenshire Railway or Tramroad Company and for other purposes" '. C.W. Nevill, the local MP, and the person with most shares present, took the chair, and after discussion the proprietors unanimously approved the Bill.

The Llanelly & Mynydd Mawr Railway Act was passed on 19th July, 1875 (38 & 39 Victoria, Cap. clxiv). The authorised share capital was now £60,000 in £10 shares, with additional powers to borrow up to £20,000. The railway was described as 12 miles 5 furlongs 2 chains and 42 links in length, commencing 'at a point about forty four yards south of the sluice gates at the south-east corner of the scouring reservoir which belongs to the Llanelly Harbour and Burry Navigation Commissioners, and is situate on the west side of the Carmarthenshire Dock' and terminating on the site of the Carmarthenshire Railway or Tramroad 66 yards due east 'from the point at which the said . . . Railway or Tramroad crossed the turnpike road leading from Swansea to Carmarthen.'

A connection was to be made with the GWR near Old Castle, and accordingly special provisions were incorporated into the Act for the protection of the GWR and traffic on the South Wales main line. These included a requirement that the L & MMR should cross the main line 'by means of a bridge with two spans or openings, each span to be of a clear width of not less than twenty-eight feet measured at right angles with the said railway, and with a clear headway for the whole distance of not less than fourteen feet six inches.' The GWR was given the right to ask for the L & MMR to build a third span of similar size, and with an eye to possible expansion in the future it also gained the right to make additional openings on either side of the bridge for further sidings. Later clauses gave protection to the property of the Llanelly Harbour Commissioners, and that of Edward Nunes Phillips of Aelybryn, near Furnace. Another clause prohibited the L & MMR from interfering with the traffic of Messrs Nevill, Druce & Co., or with traffic to or from the Old Castle colliery at Llanelly. As C.W. Mansel Lewis and the Stradey estate had the use of part of the Carmarthenshire Railway's alignment to the Carmarthenshire Dock, the Act also prevented the new company from interfering with such rights. The effect of these clauses was to ensure that the route of the L & MMR in Llanelly would run several feet to the east of the old Carmarthenshire line, at least as far north as Old Castle colliery. Beyond that point a new alignment was required around Furnace, avoiding Mr Phillips' property and the road crossings at Furnace Gate. Other portions of the route further north were also realigned to reduce the severity of some of the tramroad curves.

The 1875 Act gave the L & MMR the necessary powers to take over the Carmarthenshire Railway, but as that company's books were missing new registers of proprietors and mortgages were required before it could enter into agreements with the L & MMR, and transfer property to it. Recognising the difficulties involved in sorting out the affairs of the old company, a clause was included to allow all questions arising to be settled by a majority vote of those attending any special general assembly of proprietors. The Act also permitted the L & MMR to carry passengers and animals, as well as goods and minerals, and an elaborate scale of tolls was laid down. The relevant clauses (sections 32 to 41) are reproduced in Appendix Two.

Under the Act, Charles William Nevill, Benjamin Jones, Samuel Bevan, Joshua Wedge Buckley and Henry Rees were named as the first Directors of the new company. At their first Board meeting held in Llanelly on 6th August, 1875, Nevill was elected Chairman and Jones Deputy Chairman. John Jennings was appointed company Secretary, and Robert Johnson of Messrs Stead & Johnson became the company's solicitor. No other matters of note were discussed, and it was not until 29th October that the Directors asked one of the railway's earliest supporters, William Rosser, a local mining engineer, to draft a prospectus for the undertaking. He was also asked to contact Messrs Kinipple & Morris, civil engineers of Westminster, to prepare a detailed estimate of construction costs. The project was making progress, and although it was to take some time to develop, at long last the reconstruction of the Carmarthenshire Railway was in prospect.

The Mynydd Mawr line at Cwm Blawd in 1987. The original Carmarthenshire Railway route at this point followed the line of trees across the picture, and after reconstruction as a locomotive line a short siding was laid on this site for local traffic.   *Author*

North Dock, Llanelly, 15th June, 1962.   *Michael Hale*

View from River Lliedi Bridge at Old Castle towards the junction with the South Wales main line. The rusted and overgrown rails in the foreground were once part of the Stradey estate line. The rising grassy bank beyond the tracks is the site of the L & MM line to Llanelly Docks; May, 1987.   *Author*

Llanelly station in 1931, note the tall wooden post signals.   *Oakwood Collection*

Old Castle Crossing on 26th July, 1960, with one of the Nevill Druce Peckett tank engines waiting to go across the South Wales main line. Note the abutment for the former L&MM bridge over the main line to the docks.   *Michael Hale*

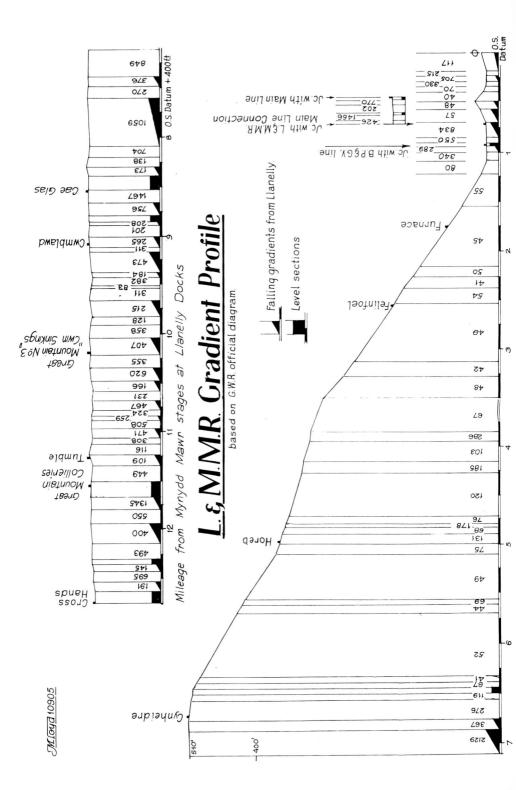

L. & M.M.R. Gradient Profile

based on G.W.R. official diagram.

JM.Lloyd 10905

Chapter Five
Rebuilding the line

The first shareholders' meeting of the L&MMR took place at Llanelly Town Hall on 18th January, 1876. By that time two important documents had been prepared. The first considered the prospects for mineral production in the district served by the new company, and revealed much about the motivation of the line's promoters. This report may be found in *Appendix Four*.

The second document was a revised estimate of construction costs. Messrs Kinipple & Morris, civil engineers of Westminster, had assessed the scheme in two sections, the first being from the junction with the GWR to Cross Hands, and the other being from the Old Castle Tin Works to the harbour. The cost of the first section was put at £52,175, including land, bridges, the relaying of the Mansel Lewis railway and the construction of goods and engine sheds. The second section was estimated to cost £3,982, including the provision of an iron bridge over the GWR.

The ensuing weeks were taken up with negotiations with the numerous interested parties. On 5th May, 1876, Messrs Kinipple & Morris, together with one of the railway's promoters, William Rosser, were formally appointed engineers for the construction of the line for fees and expenses not exceeding 5 per cent of the total outlay. At the same time C.W. Mansel Lewis, by now the owner of the Stradey estate, became Deputy Chairman. The Board also approved agreements with both the GWR and the LR&D, replacing the provisional agreements signed before the passing of the 1875 Act. The agreement with the Great Western restated arrangements for the junction near Old Castle, and included a clause to the effect that accommodation and facilities granted by the GWR should not be used in a hostile way against them, nor should such rights be transferred 'to any other company or person'. The agreement with the Llanelly Railway required the L&MM not to promote or aid an extension or branch to or from their line in the direction of the LR&D's Mountain branch to Cross Hands for a period of 21 years.

The appointment of a contractor to build the railway proved to be much more difficult than anyone expected, almost certainly because subscriptions to the new company were inadequate. J.E. Billups of Cardiff was the first contractor to be approached, in August 1876, but initially he was not able to help. The next, Charles Chambers, had offices under the same Westminster roof as Messrs Kinipple & Morris, and on 17th July, 1877, the Board was told that he was willing to tackle the job for £50,000 paid by monthly instalments in cash, the land being provided by the company. This proposal was linked to a scheme devised by one George Owen of London to take debentures under certain conditions. As the Board could not accept Owen's scheme the whole arrangement fell apart.

Messrs Kinipple & Morris now obtained estimates from a Mr Dickson – very possibly the same Mr Dickson who was then reviving the fortunes of the historic Oystermouth Railway, later known as the Swansea & Mumbles Railway. He produced figures for the construction of only nine miles of the

L & MMR railway at first, and also excluded the section over the GWR to the docks. In view of the company's lack of capital it was suggested that only half the payments should be made in cash, with the rest being paid in shares and debentures. Even so, in April 1878 the Directors felt unable to accept and the proposal lapsed. Similarly in June 1878, when at long last Mr. Billups' tender was received it was unacceptable.

The next contractors approached were Messrs Bartlett & Co. Early in 1879 the Directors were informed that they were willing to construct the line for £20,000 in cash, £20,000 in shares and £20,000 in debentures, interest on which had to be guaranteed by one of the main railway companies. Although this offer was more attractive, the last condition threatened the independence of the L & MMR. After some involved negotiations, the Board agreed amended terms on 1st April, 1879. Perhaps the date was significant: two days later the Directors rescinded their decision, and further discussion with Messrs Bartlett proved fruitless. The usual financial difficulties en-sured that some other negotiations, with a Mr Dixon of Worcester, lasted less than a month!

By the autumn of 1879 there was an air of desperation in the boardroom. The five years allowed for construction under the 1875 Act were slipping away, and the Directors had nothing to show for it. With heavy hearts they advised the shareholders to abandon the venture, and at a shareholders' meeting on 31st October, 1879, the necessary resolution was carried by 225 votes to 165. A few days later, on 4th November, the Board instructed their solicitors, Messrs Johnson & Stead, to obtain the Act of abandonment 'pro-vided they will undertake such Act at a cost not exceeding £400.'

As night is said to be darkest just before dawn, so the Mynydd Mawr Railway came closest to extinction just before its construction began. The first half of November 1879, witnessed an astonishing transformation in the company's prospects. On 12th November a letter from Messrs Kinipple & Morris was read to the Board. It discussed not the abandonment Bill, but rather a Bill to extend time for the construction of the railway! Much encouraged by the contents, it was resolved at once that the shareholders be asked to rescind their decision of 31st October.

It appears that when the shareholders met they also received a letter from the Dynant Colliery Company situated near Pontyberem, but having proper-ty extending to the proposed line of railway. The letter revealed that the Dynant company's output of about 40 tons per day was increasing, and that they would wish to use the L & MMR to move most of their coal. Furth-ermore, it was pointed out that the Brondini brickworks was under construc-tion within 100 yards of the line, and when completed it would be turning out large quantities of bricks for transport by rail. All this news filled the shareholders with fresh enthusiasm, and they promptly resolved to go to Parliament for an Act granting an extension of time to complete the project.

Notwithstanding the Dynant Colliery Co.'s letter, the main reason for this dramatic turn of events was the unexpected interest of John Waddell & Sons, a well known Scottish firm of contractors. Born in 1828 near Airdrie, by 1879 John Waddell had successfully constructed numerous lines in Scot-land, the north-east of England, and East Anglia. Although some of these had

Sandy Yard, Llanelly, seen here on 4th September, 1957.   *Michael Hale*

A view looking north at Sandy, with the site of Sandy locomotive shed on the right, on 4th September, 1957.   *Michael Hale*

involved substantial civil engineering works (for example, the Sunderland & Monkwearmouth Railway) John Waddell had not previously been involved in any important contracts in Wales. Even so, he was as welcome to the hard pressed Directors of the Mynydd Mawr as ever a lifeline was to a drowning man. By 11th December a petition for the time extension Bill was being sealed, and the contractor was being invited to meet the Board. By 22nd December the Directors were advised that Mr. Waddell was willing to construct the line for £60,000, taking £25,000 in cash and £35,000 in shares, which figures included level crossings, sidings, bridges and stations, and the relaying of the Mansel Lewis line. Accordingly Messrs Kinipple & Morris were asked to prepare specifications to enable the company to reach an agreement with the contractors.

The whole project was now revitalised, and the year 1880 began as it was to continue – with hectic activity. On 8th January the Directors and John Waddell met at the Westminster offices of Messrs Kinipple & Morris, and Mr Waddell amended his terms to ask for payment to be £30,000 in cash, and £30,000 in shares. As this offer was to be open only until 15th February both the shareholders and the Board had meetings on 12th January, as a result of which it was resolved to enter into a provisional agreement based upon the terms agreed in London. By 2nd February a new prospectus for shares had been issued and advertised, and the following day it was decided to supply Mr Waddell with a draft contract and to assure him that 'the Directors are doing all they can to place the remaining shares.'

The immediate response to the prospectus must have been less than overwhelming, because on 9th February the Directors decided to enter into a contract 'subject to their succeeding in placing the share capital within a limited time' or (and this was surely said tongue in cheek) 'failing this, Mr Waddell to take the unplaced shares himself.' From the outset there can be little doubt that John Waddell saw the potential of both the L&MMR and of the local coal industry, and was willing to risk money on both. It is less clear how such a struggling company managed to overcome all the difficulties to the satisfaction of the contractor. Rather curiously, the influential company Chairman, C.W. Mansel Lewis, does not appear to have featured in the process.

Throughout the negotiations with Waddell's, the Deputy Chairman, Casameyer William Gaussen, was in the chair, and on 18th February he was formally made Chairman with Samuel Bevan as his deputy. Not long after, on 5th March, an extraordinary meeting of shareholders approved the acquisition of shares in the old Carmarthenshire Railway in accordance with the 1875 Act, and also authorised the Directors to enter into the construction contract. John Waddell & Sons also gave their approval, and the agreement was sealed on 27th March, 1880. It provided for a single line throughout, with certain additional lines and sidings. Most of the route followed the alignment of the Carmarthenshire Railway but as this was occupied by the Stradey estate line from Old Castle to Cille (or Kille) colliery, it was planned to lay the L&MMR alongside, but a few feet further east. There was also a deviation to the south at Furnace, and other shorter deviations further north to ease some of the curves for example, at Horeb and Cwm Blawd. The contract included not only the bridge and junction with the GWR, but also two goods sheds costing not less than £130 each, a locomotive shed for two engines costing not less than £150, and two water tanks.

The L&MMR Act, 1880, extending the time for the building of the railway by three years was passed in June 1880. Waddell's jumped the starting gun, however, and work actually began on Monday 26th April, at Caerelms, near Sandy. In the words of the *Llanelly & County Guardian* 'there was no manner of ceremony whatever, but the men in workman like manner set about excavating.' Another group of men started work at Pentrepoeth, near Furnace, and steps were taken to lay a temporary single line as far as Quarry Mawr, to enable stone to be brought down to Llanelly for building purposes. On 4th May the Directors learned that the contractor had commenced 'cutting up the road near Sandy' and felt obliged to say that they would not hold themselves responsible for the consequences. They also reminded him of the need for precautions to protect the public, a point underlined in July when a boy playing near Cille lost a leg when struck by moving empty wagons.

By September it was said that five miles of line had been laid and that the contractor was 'pushing on with the works very vigorously.' At a Board meeting held on 27th September William Rosser reported on a proposed agreement with the Old Castle Iron & Tinplate Co., for the relaying and realignment of part of their line as well as the Mansel Lewis private railway. The minute of this meeting is far from clear, but it seems to suggest that the Old Castle Tinplate Co. had a line running south from their works to meet the tracks of Nevill, Druce & Co. near the South Wales main line. In addition it appears that Nevill, Druce & Co. had their own connection with the Stradey estate line at Old Castle, which they are believed to have worked by arrangement with, and on behalf of, C.W. Mansel Lewis. Unfortunately no satisfactory plan has come to light to show the situation at this date clearly, but it is known that, in June 1875, C.W. Mansel Lewis had leased the Old Castle colliery to Messrs Nevill. This lease included an old tramroad serving the disused Erw colliery a short distance east of Old Castle. Recognising that the construction of the L&MMR would deprive them of access to this old colliery, Messrs Nevill obtained a lease of other land in lieu.

The building of the L&MMR also reduced the land available for the other lines, giving rise to considerable discussion with the parties involved. In due course it was agreed that the L&MM and the Old Castle Iron & Tinplate Co. (OCI&T) should use a widened bridge over the River Lliedi new cut, and that the western side would become OCI&T property. Thereafter it seems that Nevill's railway ended south of the bridge, and the Mansel Lewis line had a separate alignment north of it, although with its own connection to the L&MMR south of it, presumably reached by way of a short section of Iron & Tinplate Company's track over the bridge. The chief questions in continuing negotiations here were whether the tinplate works would have a direct connection with the L&MM, and whether satisfactory wayleaves would be reserved to Mr Mansel Lewis. The debate dragged on for two years, until an agreement between the OCI&T Co. and the L&MMR was signed on 7th May, 1883.

On 2nd December, 1880, the *Llanelly & County Guardian* described a visit just made to the L & MMR works. At Cross Hands progress was being made in connecting the new line with Messrs Norton's colliery by way of a short branch actually financed by the contractors themselves. Further south, the permanent way was in position up to Cwm Blawd. The reporter then rode down the line on a locomotive accompanied by the cashier who had a bag of money with which to pay men at different sites along the line. As he travelled the reporter became well aware of the railway's limitations. Estimating speed at no more than 15 mph, he declared 'It is a very great mistake that many more diversions were not made from the original track of the old tramway to prevent the serpentine course of the present railway. Some of the turns are extremely sharp, and for fast travelling . . . further diversions will have to be made.' However, in a reference to a plan to build a short branch towards the centre of Llanelly, the reporter said 'This is a step in the right direction.'

The proposed branch was the Llanelly Town branch, authorised in 1881 by Board of Trade certificate under the Railways (Construction) Facilities Act, 1864, and amending Act of 1870. The company papers are not explicit about the reasons for the project, but almost certainly it expressed hopes for a passenger service over the L & MMR running into the town centre. The total length of the branch was intended to be 3 furlongs 1.65 chains, leaving the main line 300 yds north of the Old Castle Tinplate Works level crossing by a junction facing Sandy. After a curve of just 7½ chains radius, the line crossed and re-crossed the river Lliedi before reaching a terminus north of the road junction between Old Castle Road and Salamanca Road, near the Moriah chapel.

Having obtained powers to build the branch, the Directors were faced with the harder reality of paying for it. On 30th October, 1882, John Waddell attended a Board meeting and estimated that the land alone would cost £10,000, and the stations, signals, platforms etc. would cost another £6,000. He reckoned that an additional telegraph wire would be £150, and curves and guard rails equivalent to four miles of single track would amount to £3,850, making £20,000 in total. As the company's most immediate concern was to find funds to pay for its main line, the plans for the Town branch were put on one side.

In the 1880s there was a persistent belief in Llanelly and district that the London & North Western Railway would buy out either the BP & GVR or the L & MMR, or both. The idea originated in the early 1870s, when the LNWR assumed control of the former Llanelly Railway route from Llandilo to Carmarthen, and attempts were made to build the Burry Port & North Western Junction Railway (BP & NWJ) north to Llanarthney. A proposal for this line in 1872 did not make much progress, but in 1881 Parliamentary approval was given to a new presentation of the BP & NWJ scheme. On this occasion it was intended to drop a line down the hillside from Cwm Blawd on the L & MMR to make a connection with the proposed extension from the BP & GVR near Cwmmawr. The junction at Llanarthney again faced east, although a slightly shorter route was proposed near Porthyrhyd. The initial reaction of the Mynydd Mawr Directors in January 1881 was to ask their

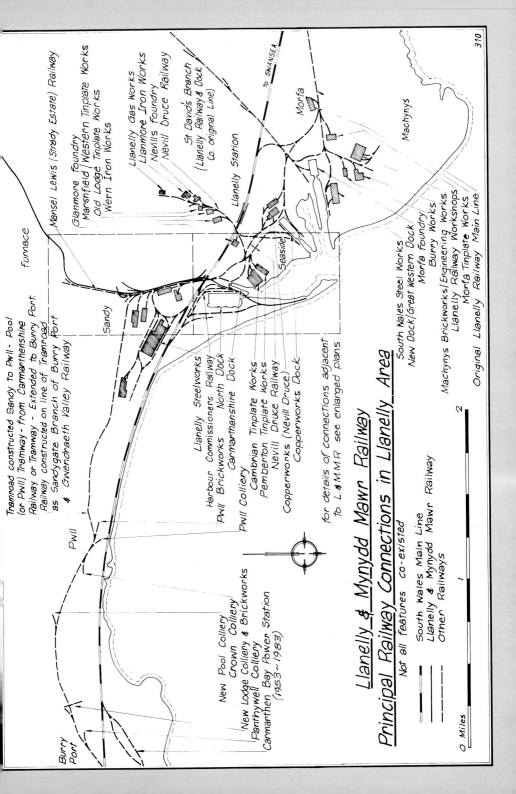

Llanelly & Mynydd Mawr Railway
Principal Railway Connections in Llanelly Area

Not all features co-existed

Tramroad constructed Sandy to Pwll - Pool (or Pwll) Tramway - from Carmarthenshire Railway or Tramway - Extended to Burry Port. Railway constructed on line of Tramroad as Sandygate Branch of Burry Port & Gwendraeth Valley Railway

Furnace

Mansel Lewis (Stradey Estate) Railway

Glanmore Foundry
Marshfield/Western Tinplate Works
Old Lodge Tinplate Works
Wern Iron Works

Llanelly Gas Works
Llanmore Iron Works
Nevills Foundry
Nevill Druce Railway

St David's Branch
(Llanelly Railway & Dock
Co. original Line)

Llanelly Station

Morfa

Machynys

to SWANSEA

Seaside

Sandy

Pwll

Llanelly Steelworks
Harbour Commissioners Railway
Pwll Brickworks
Carmarthenshire Dock
North Dock
Pwll Colliery
Cambrian Tinplate Works
Pemberton Tinplate Works
Nevill Druce Railway
Copperworks (Nevill Druce)
Copperworks Dock

for details of connections adjacent to L.& M.M.R see enlarged plans

South Wales Steel Works
New Dock/Great Western Dock
Morfa Foundry
Burry Works
Machynys Brickworks/Engineering Works
Llanelly Railway Workshops
Morfa Tinplate Works
Original Llanelly Railway Main Line

New Pool Colliery
Crown Colliery
New Lodge Colliery & Brickworks
Panthywell Colliery
Carmarthen Bay Power Station
(1953~1983)

Burry Port

South Wales Main Line
Llanelly & Mynydd Mawr Railway
Other Railways

0 Miles   1   2

310

Sandy Junction, Llanelly, with 0−6−0PT No. 1666 coming off the BP&GVR branch on 26th July, 1960.   *Michael Hale*

The same scene at Sandy seen in 1987 now very much devoid of trackwork.   *Author*

solicitors to draft clauses protective of the company. The following month the solicitors attended the Parliamentary committee considering the Bill, ready to petition against it. In March, however, the Board withdrew its opposition on the understanding that an undertaking would be given for forwarding traffic to and from the L&MMR. Ironically, on 1st July, 1881, the BP&GVR went into receivership, and although the Bill was passed little or nothing was done to put it into effect.

In 1881 there was additional evidence of the contractor's commitment to the Mynydd Mawr company. In January the Board heard a proposal for Waddell's to work the railway for five years for a diminishing proportion of the receipts – the contractors receiving 70 per cent in the first year, 60 per cent in the second year, and 50 per cent in the remaining three years. This was accepted, subject to Waddell's being ready to guarantee interest payments on the company's debentures. John Waddell & Sons agreed.

As railway construction continued apace, John Waddell proposed to build coal shipping stages for the L&MMR near the Carmarthenshire Dock, and to find the money himself. An editorial in the *Llanelly & County Guardian* on 19th May, 1881, making unflattering comparisons with the Llanelly Harbour Commissioners, observed 'It is gratifying to learn that one at least acts as if he had confidence in the future prospects of our Harbour and backs it up by action. We refer to Mr Waddell, the energetic and enterprising contractor of the Mynydd Mawr Railway.' In fact the Directors did not approve plans for the coal stages and adjoining railway sidings until March 1882,and only one stage was built that year.

On 26th May, 1881, the newspaper was advertising a Whit Monday excursion over the L&MMR to celebrate the completion of the line. As there were numerous items of work outstanding this was premature, and also almost certainly lacking Board of Trade consent. When the advert stated 'The tea ticket includes the travelling by train,' it was probably hinting at the illegality. At any rate, on 9th June the newspaper described how, a few days earlier, on the 6th, by courtesy of the contractor and the officials of the Mynydd Mawr Railway, '1000 souls' were conveyed to Cross Hands for a large picnic party. The Furnace district 'was gay with bunting' and people waved flags from windows. The first train of 16 wagons left the Furnace at 11.30 am, 'preceded by two engines nicely decorated with evergreens, and the train was accompanied by the New Dock fife and drum band which played lively strains on the way up. A second train left about 12.30 pm with about eight trucks, and all were deposited safely at Cross Hands where solid and liquid intoxicants were provided . . .' After sports and amusements were enjoyed, the evening trains were expected to return at 8.00 pm and 10.00 pm. The train which departed at 8.10 pm 'took 2 hours 20 minutes to return causing anxiety to the waiting company – but at 10.15 pm the whistle was heard as the train unloaded people at Felin Foel.' Ironically, at the time of this excursion the L&MMR had not completed its purchase of the old Carmarthenshire Railway. This was approved by the shareholders in August 1881, for the sum of £1,397 3s. 0d., and the transaction was completed that December.

In July 1881, the *Llanelly & County Guardian* recorded two likely 'firsts', and also the running of another passenger train. What was probably the first death on the works was reported early in the month when a small child fell from the unfinished railway bridge near the Carmarthenshire Dock. The other 'first' was far happier – the first consignment of goods over the L&MMR, being a wagon load of flour from John Randell of Llanelly forwarded to Cwm Blawd for Mr Greville of Pontyberem. On Saturday 9th July, William Rosser invited the Chairman of the Board of Health and the Chairman of the Harbour Commissioners to accompany him and a number of others on a trip over the line. Starting from Sandy, Mr Rosser pointed out the features *en route*. 'The Swiss Valley was the admiration of all the party, as was also the Llanelly New Waterworks, with its fine sheet of water extending some mile and a half up the valley.' To judge from the glowing press report this piece of public relations was highly successful.

It seems very likely that Waddell's accepted local goods traffic on an *ad hoc* basis from July 1881, onwards. The railway certainly saw some activity. In May 1882, for example, the local newspaper reported how two ballast trucks had become uncontrollable, and had 'fled down the line at a rattling pace, coming into contact with an empty truck near the Furnace, which was smashed up, fortunately causing no further injury.' Earlier, in February 1882, whilst the Directors proposed that their formal working agreement with the contractor should commence on the day the railway opened for public traffic, they added that 'as the company assume he is taking public traffic they would like . . . to avoid future misunderstanding (by knowing) from what date he considers the line open.' In April John Waddell replied by saying that the railway would be open when the branch to Norton's colliery at Cross Hands was open. This branch was another instance of the contractor's initiative, because although the L&MMR was obliged by its agreement with the Llanelly Railway not to extend towards the Mountain branch, the contractors were not so restricted. Indeed they really cocked a snook at the Llanelly Railway, because their private branch not only linked the old Cross Hands colliery and Gorsgoch colliery with the L&MMR, but it was also extended alongside the Mountain branch to serve Gilfach colliery as well. By August 1881, however, the L&MMR and Messrs Norton were discussing a draft agreement for working colliery traffic, and at the same time the railway company had reached an agreement with Waddell's regarding the junction near Cross Hands.

Quite apart from the Norton's (or Gilfach) branch, there were several other matters hindering the official opening of the railway. First, the arrangements being made with the Mansel Lewis line and the Old Castle Iron & Tinplate Co. had not been completed. Secondly, although on 11th January, 1882, the Llanelly Harbour Commissioners granted a lease to the L&MMR giving access to the Carmarthenshire Dock, and new shipping berths nearby, the coal shipping stages were not then built. Thirdly, negotiations were continuing with the GWR concerning the junction near Old Castle. Although a draft agreement was approved by the L&MMR on 5th April, 1882, it was not until 24th July that the company Secretary, John Jennings, signed an undertaking to the GWR in respect of temporary works at the junction. The arrangements were confirmed by a formal agreement sealed on 30th December, 1882, subject to the conditions that on three months notice from the

Sandy locomotive shed seen in August 1931. On the left is No. 312 and on the right No. 2011.   *J. Lowe*

The site of the original L&MMR engine shed near Cille, north of Sandy, seen on 6th November, 1987.   *Author*

GWR the road bridge might be widened, and two sidings lengthened to accommodate up to 20 wagons. Any such alterations would be at the expense of the L&MMR, which paid £100 for the privilege of having the junction.

The question of through rates between the L&MMR and other railway companies was a further outstanding issue. In January 1882, John Waddell suggested that Samuel Mason of Edinburgh, who had some experience of railway administration, should be appointed to the Mynydd Mawr Board to deal with this topic. The Directors replied coolly, saying that there was no vacancy, and that Mr Mason could be nominated at the next annual shareholders' meeting. This took place in March, and Mr Mason was proposed. An existing Director, Mr W. Howell, objected and said (in effect) that if Mr Mason was elected John Waddell would have control of the entire company. In spite of the contractor's good work, he had been paid so much in shares as to have a very powerful position in company affairs – and this was not appreciated by all the local Directors. However, the little-known Samuel Mason seems to have joined the Board briefly, resigning in 1884. Doubtless assisted by Mr Mason, there was correspondence with the GWR about accounting for tolls with them direct rather than through the Railway Clearing House. John Waddell's views were sought, and at the same time on 10th December, 1882, the Directors declared that the railway should be considered to be open for public traffic from 1st January, 1883. This date was adhered to, but as the railway was regarded locally as being open already there was no ceremony and no apparent reference to the occasion in the press. In spite of all the negotiations, the junction with the GWR was not connected until some weeks later.

The L&MMR bridge over the Carmarthen Road, at Cross Hands, probably photographed soon after World War I.   E. Jones

Chapter Six
The Waddells take charge, 1883–1895

In 1883 the L&MMR was worked by two contractor's locomotives that had been used during the building of the line. These were tank engines, one four-coupled and the other six-coupled, built by Andrew Barclay & Co. A shed just large enough to accommodate these engines was erected at Cille, between Sandy and Furnace, but often only one engine was in steam. Indeed, the four-coupled locomotive left the line in 1885 and was not replaced until 1886. The main goods depot in Llanelly was at Sandy, and others were provided at Felin Foel, Horeb, Cynheidre, Cwm Blawd, Tumble and Cross Hands. There were passing loops at Cynheidre and Tumble, and also sidings at Quarry Mawr, north of Felin Foel, and at Dynant between Cwm Blawd and Tumble. It is not known if all of these were available for traffic when the railway was officially deemed to be open. Although minerals were always the most important freight on the line, the company was also keen to carry agricultural and other goods required by the small communities served by the railway. As a freight line, no signalling was provided, and all trains were operated on a time interval basis.

The finances of the L&MMR were in a mess in 1883. The company owed at least £6,000 to the contractor, and smaller sums to many others. The Chairman, C.W. Gaussen, resigned in May, and a semblance of respectability was maintained by the appointment of Sir John Jones Jenkins in his place. By August, however, Messrs Johnson & Stead, the solicitors, had seen the condition of the company and had decided to retain the L&MM's deeds and documents 'as their Bill of Costs was unpaid.' In March 1884, when a bill of £200 had to be paid, the Board resolved that a cheque should be drawn but not paid until the receipt of certain calls on shares.

This hand to mouth existence was not assisted by traffic returns on the new line. In many parts of South Wales traffic flourished as soon as a railway was opened. This was not the case with the L&MMR. In the first six months to the end of June 1883, only 3,822 train miles were run – or roughly equivalent to one return trip over the line five days per week. At the annual meeting of shareholders on 28th February, 1884, it was reported that traffic for the half-year to the end of December was little more than the previous six months. At the same time it was announced that arrangements were being made to bring coal from the Dynant colliery over the company's line, with the assertion that if this were done 'there would be a considerable increase in the revenue of the company.'

Sir John Jones Jenkins as Chairman regretted that the report was not more satisfactory, adding 'that several things had occurred in connection with the railway which had not been foreseen by those who took part in promoting the scheme.' He pointed out that the anthracite trade had been exceedingly bad, and that some of the collieries from which they had anticipated traffic had ceased working. This situation must have been well known to the local press, but in August 1885, this did not prevent the *Llanelly & County Guardian* from publishing an enthusiastic account of the mineral potential of Mynydd Mawr, adding that 'At the end of the line near Mynydd Mawr are

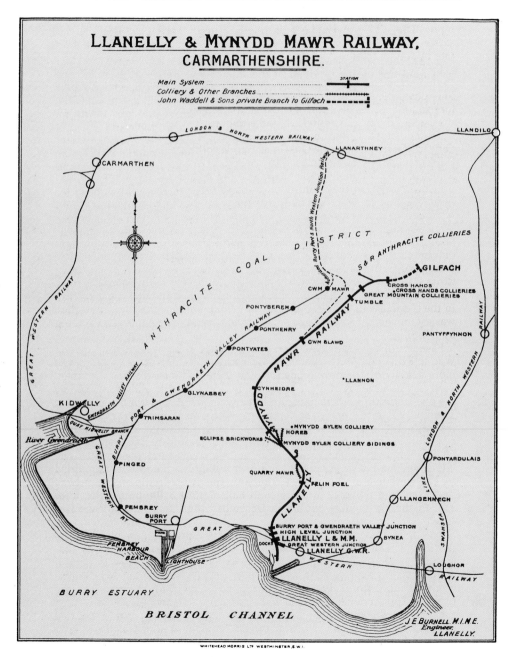

From the *Great Western Railway Magazine* (1923) – see page 77.

collieries called Gorsgoch and Cross Inn [sic], the former belonging to representatives of the late Mr B. Jones, Caeffair. These collieries were in existence 50 years ago, and have for a part of the time produced coal at the rate of 100 to 150 tons per day.'

By this time the Gilfach colliery had closed, probably in 1883. Trade was so depressed that some anthracite producers preferred to collaborate rather than compete, seeking to maintain prices as far as possible. At this period, for example, Messrs Norton of Cross Hands often exchanged information on the state of the market with C.R. Vickerman of the Bonvilles Court Coal Co., at Saundersfoot. Unfortunately such arrangements were not of lasting benefit to Messrs Norton: the Old Cross Hands colliery was closed in 1887, the Gorsgoch colliery having closed by the end of 1885.

Just as John Waddell & Sons had been the saviours of the Mynydd Mawr project in 1879, so they continued to be through all the difficulties of the decade. By agreeing to take half their payment for the work in shares, they were also accepting a dominant role in the company's affairs. Whatever John Waddell thought of the local directorate, there can be little doubt that he had faith in the potential of the Mynydd Mawr district. From the outset he was determined to see his investment succeed. Although his first attempt to bring coal traffic on to the line over the Norton's, or Gilfach extension at Cross Hands was thwarted by pit closures, John Waddell was not deterred. He spent a further £3,000 on forming a connection with the Dynant colliery in the Gwendraeth valley. Unfortunately not very long after the connection was established – by way of a rope-worked incline – the colliery was closed by flooding.

Faced with such setbacks, a lesser man might well have withdrawn. John Waddell did not. With characteristic courage, he decided to spend even more heavily on the development of the Mynydd Mawr district. Prompted partly by assurances of dock improvements at Llanelly, and even more by his own refusal to countenance failure, he acquired mineral leases around Tumble. The most important comprised 292 acres around Danygraig farm, leased in 1886. The Great Mountain Anthracite Collieries Co. was formed, and work began on sinking the mine. The colliery opened in 1887, and by 1892 it employed 600 men and had an output of about 400 tons per day. The village of Tumble grew rapidly, and over a hundred homes were provided for the workmen by the colliery company. Inevitably traffic on the railway increased, and whereas in the second half of 1884 5,400 train miles were run, in the six months ending in December 1887, the train mileage was 11,467.

The opening of the Great Mountain colliery marked a new phase in the development of the L&MMR, although the improvement was not instantaneous. In November 1887, the company was in such a parlous state that it could not afford to pay for some local newspaper adverts! Even more importantly for the future, the Board recognised that it could not afford the Llanelly Town branch, and resolved to abandon it. However, by this time it must have been obvious to everyone that Waddell's were in charge, and that even if the Mynydd Mawr company was impoverished, it was unlikely to founder. Indeed, by the mid-1880s it appears that local interest had waned,

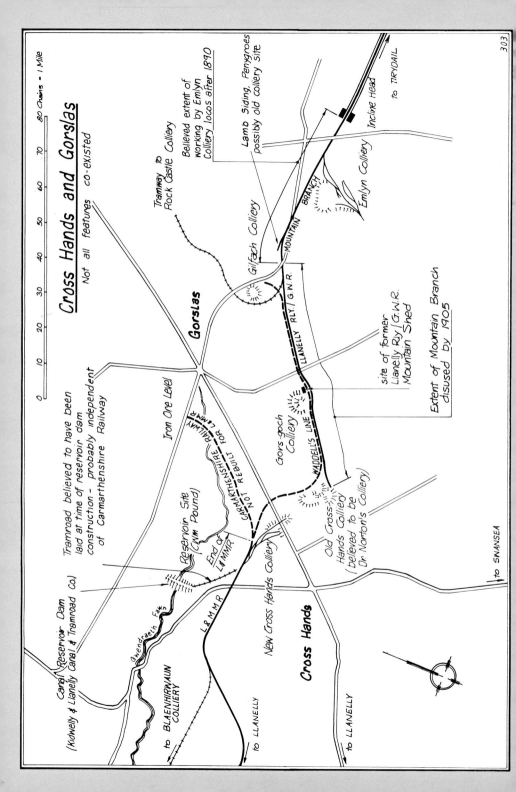

Cross Hands and Gorslas

Not all features co-existed

80 Chains = 1 Mile

0 10 20 30 40 50 60 70

303

Canal Reservoir Dam
(Kidwelly & Llanelly Canal & Tramroad Co.)

Tramroad believed to have been laid at time of reservoir dam construction - probably independent of Carmarthenshire Railway

Iron Ore Level

Gorslas

Tramway to Rock Castle Colliery

Believed extent of working by Emlyn Colliery locos after 1890

Lamb Siding, Penygroes possibly old colliery site

Emlyn Colliery Incline Head

to TIRYDAIL

Gilfach Colliery

MOUNTAIN   BRANCH

LLANELLY RLY / G.W.R.

site of former Llanelly Rly / G.W.R. Mountain Shed

Extent of Mountain Branch disused by 1905

Reservoir Site (CWM POUND)

CARMARTHENSHIRE RAILWAY FOR L&MMR NOT REBUILT

End of L&MMR

Gwendraeth Fâch

BLAENHIRWAUN COLLIERY

L & M M R

to LLANELLY

New Cross Hands Colliery

Gors-goch Colliery

WADDELL'S LINE

Old Cross Hands Colliery (believed to be Dr Norton's Colliery)

Cross Hands

to LLANELLY

to SWANSEA

and that most people were content to leave the L&MMR to John Waddell. There were certainly some changes amongst the company Directors at this period, and there is a completely unexplained gap in the company records between 1885 and 1887. Suffice to say that early supporters of the railway like Samuel Bevan, William Howell, Henry Rees and John Randell left the Board, and instead friends of John Waddell like Samuel Mason, and later William Maitland Stewart joined it. Stewart was actually Chairman briefly in 1887, before he resigned and was replaced as a Director by W.J. Wilson. The Chairman of the Board from October 1887, was George Blake, agent to C.W. Mansel Lewis.

In spite of all the attention John Waddell gave to the L&MMR, it is important to recognise that he continued to have contracting interests in other parts of the country. In 1881, for example, he took on a major contract to build a tunnel under the River Mersey for the Mersey Railway. As with the Mynydd Mawr line, Waddell agreed to help finance the project provided he was given a free hand to control administration, design and construction. Unfortunately, in 1887 the Mersey Railway went into receivership, and almost certainly gave John Waddell some financial headaches. However he remained entirely faithful to the L&MM line, because on 14th November, 1887, he sealed a new 10 year working agreement with the company.

This agreement came into effect on 1st January, 1888, and it provided a clear statement of the realities of life on the Mynydd Mawr. It required the company to provide the railway, and the contractor to provide the locomotives, rolling stock and staff to work it. Under the agreement Waddell's received 1d. per ton on all traffic using their plant at Llanelly harbour, and also 60 per cent of the remainder of the gross receipts. The company received the other 40 per cent. However, the most significant provision was that empowering the contractor to use the company's name, and to fix tolls, rates and charges. In this sense, by 1887, the distinction between the two parties was really only technical. Although the L&MMR had other shareholders, John Waddell & Sons were clearly in charge.

John Waddell had the satisfaction of seeing both the L&MMR and the Great Mountain colliery become established, but he did not witness any further development. He died in Edinburgh on 17th January, 1888, aged 59. A man of vision and dynamism in the great age of railway construction, his energy and experience were much missed. He was succeeded by his son George, and whilst the Mynydd Mawr's records hardly allow for a fair assessment, it would seem that he was not in quite the same mould as his father. John's grandsons, Robert and John junior became partners in the contracting business after they reached their majority.

When the Burry Port & North Western Junction was originally proposed the coal industry was booming right across South Wales, and there can be little doubt that the LNWR was keen to extend its influence to the Mynydd Mawr, the Gwendraeth Valley and the coast. By the mid 1880s the LNWR's interest in the anthracite coalfield was less certain, although many in Llanelly and district still believed it to be real. An editorial in the *Llanelly & County Guardian* for 20th January. 1887, clearly articulated local opinion. Claiming 'with some authority' that the 'powerful and enterprising' LNWR

A scene within the confines of the Eclipse brickworks at Horeb at the turn of the century.

was negotiating for the purchase of Pembrey Old Dock, and the BP&GVR, the newspaper declared,

> We are sure it must come to this 'ere long seeing the L&NW would thereby have a port of their own in the British Channel, which, it is said, they have been longingly casting their eyes about to acquire for some time. The purchase afterwards of the Mynydd Mawr Railway and the extension of the line to Llanarthney would put in the hands of this company the mineral products in coal, iron and limestone of a very rich and extensive district, which they could ship within easy distance by their own lines. Moreover the starting of mineral industries would increase the population of the district, which would call for railway passenger accomodation likewise.

The issues of harbour facilities was always a consideration in the BP &NWJ proposals. Up to 1882 the L&MMR's dealings with the Llanelly Harbour Commissioners were entirely amicable, but in 1883 the Commissioners disputed John Waddell's account for works in connection with the Mynydd Mawr stage erected near the Carmarthenshire Dock. The contractor assured them that no one could have done the work cheaper, and a settlement was reached, but this matter marked the start of a gradual deterioration in the relationship between Waddell's and the Commissioners. The channel approaching the Mynydd Mawr stage was narrow, and prone to silting. Wind off the sea often blew sand across the sidings, and into wagon axle boxes. Waddell's repeatedly pressed for improvements, and made little progress. By the late 1880s, when a considerable increase in traffic was anticipated, the contractor was becoming frustrated by the Commissioners lack of positive response.

In the meantime, a few miles to the west, the management of the BP&GVR was showing far more initiative by providing a floating dock capable of accommodating ocean-going ships of up to 1,800 tons. This was a remarkable achievement for a company in receivership, but most of the labour had been undertaken by the BP&GV's own men. Two coal tips were installed on the West Dock, with sidings laid out for the expeditious handling of traffic. When the dock was first used, on 1st October, 1888, its facilities were far superior to those available at the Harbour Commissioners' Carmarthenshire Dock in Llanelly.

By now George Waddell was the senior figure in John Waddell & Sons, and he was quick to appreciate the importance of this development at Burry Port. Almost certainly he saw the possibilities of using it for the shipment of Mynydd Mawr coal, independent of Llanelly. In 1889, no doubt wary of antagonising the Harbour Commissioners, he conducted an extremely discreet correspondence with the Board of the BP&GVR, and offered to buy their company for £96,000. Although this would have represented a loss to the shareholders, the company was effectively bankrupt, and the offer might have appeared attractive. However no transaction took place.

Instead, in 1890, the BP&GVR brought forward a scheme to provide a direct rail connection to the L&MMR by extending their Pwll branch over the route of the old tramroad to Sandy. As track was in position as far as Pwll colliery, and as they already had authority to build a line as far as Sandy Gate, the Bill sought powers to construct just 2 more chains of railway to a junction with the Mynydd Mawr 5 chains south of the Pembrey Road bridge at Sandy. The Bill also provided for the new line to cross or connect with the Mansel Lewis private railway.

The most interesting features of the Bill were provisions to enable the BP & GVR and the L & MMR to enter into agreements for the working, use, management and maintenance of the respective railways, their stock and equipment. There were also provisions for the exchange of traffic, and the fixing and collection of tolls and charges. Somewhat surprisingly, for a Bill promoted in the name of the BP & GV, it included consent for the L & MMR to abandon the Town branch, and sought to release the Mynydd Mawr from any outstanding contractual or other obligations in respect of it.

Considering the significance of this Bill, it is remarkable that the Mynydd Mawr minute books have virtually nothing to say about it. In the circumstances the Bill must be regarded as the eventual outcome of Waddell's discreet diplomacy. If this is correct, it implies that instead of taking over the BP & GVR, the contractor had opted to encourage both companies to work much more closely together, and had persuaded the BP & GVR to sponsor the necessary Bill.

At all events, the Llanelly Harbour Commissioners did not like it, regarding the developments at Burry Port as a serious threat to the prosperity of the docks at Llanelly. The opposition in Llanelly went so far as to organise public meetings to resist the proposal, and the Commissioners demanded that the BP & GVR should impose a charge of 1d. per ton on all traffic leaving the L & MMR for their line. On hearing of this in April 1891, George Waddell wrote to John Jennings, the clerk to the Commissioners to object:

> I think it is most unreasonable to ask them to agree to this, for I am satisfied once Llanelly gives facilities and this line made, there will be more traffic coming off the Burry Port line on to the Mynydd Mawr for shipment at the New Dock, Llanelly, than will leave the Mynydd Mawr for shipping at Pembrey, and surely if a New Dock is to be constructed at Llanelly it cannot lose by having another direct railway connection into same, independent of the Great Western.

In spite of the opposition, the Bill was passed. The Commissioners had no need to worry. As the BP & GV was still in receivership it had difficulty in financing the line. As with the West Dock, therefore, it employed its own staff to do the work. Such an arrangement did not make for swift progress, and in 1894 powers for the work lapsed. An extension of time was granted, and on 11th December, 1894, the L & MMR, John Waddell & Sons, and the BP & GVR were parties to an agreement for the junction at Sandy. For the easement, and the right to use the junction the Burry Port company eventually paid the Mynydd Mawr £100. In June 1895 Waddell's were asked to lay the junction and to send their bill to the BP & GVR. In view of Waddell's customary efficiency this was probably done promptly, but the BP & GVR were still struggling with their part of the work. According to a report by H. Court, the Burry Port's Engineer, in September 1898, the new railway had then been completed to within 5 furlongs of the junction with the Mynydd Mawr, and was advanced enough for a connection to be made with an offshoot of the Mansel Lewis railway known as the 'Marsh line'. The BP & GVR connection with the L & MMR was eventually opened in April 1899,

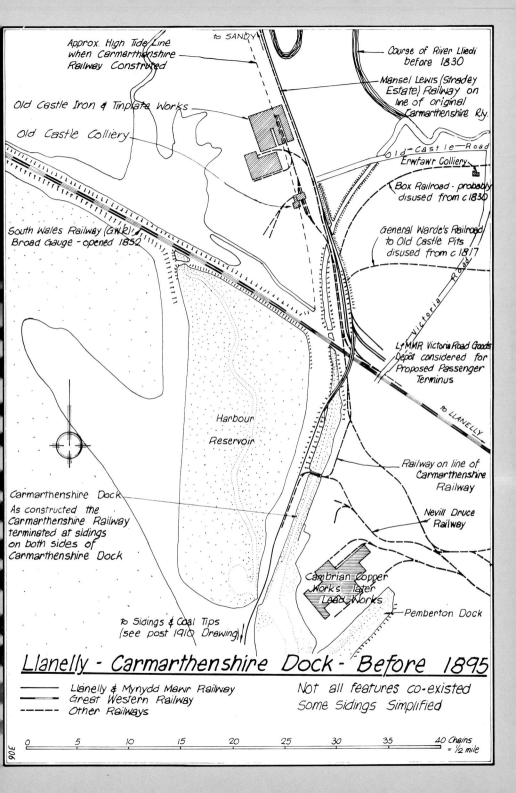

Approx. High Tide Line
when Carmarthenshire
Railway Constructed

to SANDY

Course of River Lliedi
before 1830

Mansel Lewis (Stradey
Estate) Railway on
line of original
Carmarthenshire Rly.

Old Castle Iron & Tinplate Works

Old Castle Colliery

Old Castle Road

Erwfawr Colliery

Box Railroad - probably
disused from c 1830

South Wales Railway (GWR)
Broad Gauge - opened 1852

General Warde's Railroad
to Old Castle Pits
disused from c 1817

Victoria Road

L & MMR Victoria Road Goods
Depot considered for
Proposed Passenger
Terminus

to LLANELLY

Harbour

Reservoir

Railway on line of
Carmarthenshire
Railway

Carmarthenshire Dock

Nevill Druce
Railway

As constructed the
Carmarthenshire Railway
terminated at sidings
on both sides of
Carmarthenshire Dock

Cambrian Copper
Works later
Lead Works

Pemberton Dock

to Sidings & Coal Tips
(see post 1910 Drawing)

Llanelly - Carmarthenshire Dock - Before 1895

————— Llanelly & Mynydd Mawr Railway
═══════ Great Western Railway
– – – – Other Railways

Not all features co-existed
Some Sidings Simplified

0   5   10   15   20   25   30   35   40 Chains
= ½ mile

306

and coal from the Gwendraeth valley was shipped at Llanelly soon after. Recounting this development has taken the story some way ahead of strict chronology. The willingness of John Waddell & Sons to finance shipping stages, colliery branches and rolling stock was undoubtedly an immense help to the railway company. By 1887, however, the company's own capital had been exhausted, and it was struggling even to pay interest on sums owing to numerous creditors, including the contractor. Indeed, it is believed that they held all the original (or 'A') debentures. In 1887, though, the High Court sanctioned a 'scheme of arrangement' to help both the company and its creditors. The L&MMR was authorised to create £25,000 'B' debentures, and it was hoped that these would not only help to meet the debts, but also provide some fresh capital. Thereafter the company got into the habit of issuing 'B' debentures in respect of much of its expenditure. Although most went to the contractor – for example, for laying additional sidings at Sandy in 1888 – they were even issued to the executors of William Morris, of Messrs Kinipple & Morris, who died in 1889. This procedure absorbed a growing amount of the company's income. In August 1890, for example, the company paid debenture interest of almost £1,164, having just received £1,186 from the contractor in respect of traffic worked in the previous half year!

The layout proposed for Sandy sidings in 1888 comprised 440 yds of sidings which were reckoned to be sufficient for 73 wagons. In addition, another new siding was planned for a site adjacent to the L&MM's loop before the junction with the GWR, and below the high level line to the Mynydd Mawr stage. This was to be 133 yds long, and capable of holding 18 wagons. In the event a total of 596 yds of siding were built at these sites at a cost of £2,981. Other sidings soon followed, and in July 1890, Waddell's were paid a further £1880 in 'B' debentures. In October 1891, the Board sanctioned a coal depot near Sandy, and in July 1892 Waddell's were appealing for a modern weighing machine on the site.

After the depression and the pit closures of the 1880s, the coal trade began to recover. One indication of this came in January 1890, when a Mr Llewellyn Davies requested the company's rates for coal from Cross Hands colliery to Swansea. Amazingly the Mynydd Mawr took three months to reply, but then produced rates (including tipping at the docks) which clearly favoured Llanelly – at the Mynydd Mawr stages 1s. per ton; at New Dock, Llanelly – 1s. 6d. per ton; at North and South Docks, Swansea – 2s. 2d. per ton; and at the Prince of Wales Dock, Swansea – 2s. 5d. ton. In due course mining activities at Cross Hands resumed, and in March 1893 the company developing the new Cross Hands colliery advised the L&MM of its intention to work coal under the railway. The Directors pressed for their undertaking not to work the shallower veins, and asked William Rosser, the Engineer, to advise on the likely effects of their working the deeper veins.

The L&MMR's traffic returns show clearly how business began to grow in the late 1880s. In March 1888, the company's share of the monthly receipts was £276 9s. 4d., more than double any sum previously received. Although there were noticeable fluctuations thereafter, in 1889 the L&MM's monthly share was never less than £250, and in March and December it exceeded

The BP&GUR branch to Sandy between Pwll colliery and Sandygate sidings.

R.W. Davies Collection

Pwll colliery engine house seen in November, 1987.   *Author*

A general view of Great Mountain Colliery, Tumble.   *R.E. Bowen Collection*

An early postcard view of Railway Terrace, Tumble.   *H.L. Morgan*

A view looking up Llandeilo Road, Cross Hands showing the bridge carrying a tramway from Cross Hands Colliery to a spoil tip on the site of old Cross Hands Colliery which was behind the houses on the right. Waddell's private line to Gilfach passed under the road a short distance beyond the bridge.   *Mrs W.B. James*

The huge Cross Hands Colliery tip, as seen in the 1960s.   *E. Wilkins*

£440. In October 1891, after a poor September, the share rose to £649 8s. 5d. In 1893, at a time of industrial unrest, the figures dipped considerably, but in 1894 and 1895 traffic recovered. Indeed, by 1895 the L&MMR was regularly moving 5,000 to 8,000 tons per month, and even though one locomotive was destroyed in a boiler explosion in March 1889, by the early 1890s the contractors had five others on the railway. As there was no signalling, it appears that all trains were worked on a time interval basis.

The industrial unrest in 1893 was centred on the Great Mountain Colliery at Tumble – often referred to at that time as the Tumble. When sinking the mine, the colliery company had provided over 100 homes for miners and their families, many of whom came from Scotland or the north of England. The newcomers to the village inevitably brought with them differences of culture, language and denomination. For the Welsh speaking inhabitants the dramatic expansion of their community was a profound shock. Matters were not made easier by the fact that many of the new arrivals were skilled men, qualified for some of the better jobs in the colliery.

Against this background, in 1893 the colliery company proposed a reduction in wages. Early in March the men came out, and in spite of the mediation of the famous Welsh miners' leader William Abraham ('Mabon'), the dispute dragged on. From time to time there were scuffles and skirmishes in Tumble. The colliery manager, a Scotsman named Beith, was particularly disliked. By August there was increasing bitterness between local people and outsiders. About 60 men were still at work at Great Mountain, almost all newcomers – and yet more were arriving in Tumble looking for employment. To make matters worse, David Kydd for the colliery company, attempted to give 17 tenants notice to quit.

On 4th September, 1893, this simmering brew of emotions boiled over into a riot. A large body of strikers went on the rampage through Tumble, venting their anger chiefly on the homes of management, and of the men still at work. Police reinforcements were dispatched to Tumble, by way of the L&MMR, and a detachment of the Inniskilling Dragoons encamped at the village for almost a month. By then tempers had cooled, and many newcomers had prudently decided to leave the district. After the event, the weary parties greatly regretted the violence. There was a new willingness to negotiate, and on 1st January, 1894, a settlement was reached based upon new rates for prices and wages. Unfortunately, though, this dispute did not enhance anyone's reputation. It cost Waddell's much local goodwill, whilst Tumble acquired a name for wildness which regrettably was not erased for many years.

David Kydd of the colliery company became a Director of the L&MMR in 1893. By now E.R. Fisher and Sir John Jones Jenkins (later Lord Glantawe) had resigned. W. Buckley Roderick joined the directorate in 1894, by which time Samuel Bevan was in the middle of his second period of service as a Director, lasting from 1889 to 1899. Board meetings were usually held at the company's offices at Mansfield House, Queen Victoria Road, in Llanelly. These premises were held under a tenancy agreement granted by C.W. Mansel Lewis, and in the early 1890s there was protracted negotiation with him over a new lease. The company asked William Rosser to make a valuation, and eventually a 60 year lease was sealed in August 1894. Sadly Mr Rosser died in the following year. As he had been active in public affairs since the 1860s, his death was a considerable loss to the district. It also severed another long standing link with the early days of the Llanelly & Mynydd Mawr Railway.

Cynheidre before the construction of the colliery. Note the water tank in the far distance.   *R.C. Riley*

0–6–0PT No. 1628 at Cynheidre on the same day, 3rd June, 1953.   *R.C. Riley*

A derelict view of Llanarthney Station as seen on 10th August, 1990. This was the station the L & MMR never reached.   *Author*

The line of the Caeglas colliery tramway route – the notch in the hillside marks the cutting taking the line down to the L & MMR seen on 14th December, 1989. The photograph was taken from the site of the former colliery.   *Author*

Chapter Seven
Controversy and consolidation, 1896–1906

The history of the L&MMR at the turn of the century is dominated by an extraordinary dispute between the company and the Llanelly Harbour Commissioners. It concerns the building of the North Dock, authorised by Act of Parliament in 1896. From the point of view of the Commissioners and the ratepayers of Llanelly this scheme was essential for the commercial development of the port and the town. From the viewpoint of the L&MM the construction work entailed the breach of an important agreement, and threatened the loss of access to the Mynydd Mawr stages. Strong feelings were stirred on both sides, and with the benefit (and the safety) of hindsight, it can be seen that the dispute was not only bitter and sad, but also at times quite farcical. Indeed, it was a row of such dimensions as to be the subject of the next chapter; other developments at this period are described here.

By 1896 the investment and industry of John Waddell & Sons had carried the Mynydd Mawr forward to financial stability, although not prosperity. In the absence of full accounts the true position cannot be stated with certainty, but the traffic returns do provide an indication of the company's progress. In the year 1897, for example, the L&MM's share of the monthly receipts only once fell below £400, and the monthly figure was well over £500 in each month from April to July. The Great Mountain colliery was easily the most important source of revenue – in September 1897, for instance, 9,765½ tons of coal were conveyed over the line, and only 295 tons of the total had come from Cross Hands. In the following month Cross Hands managed to dispatch over 913 tons, whilst Tumble forwarded almost 7,339 tons. In spite of these encouraging figures, George Blake, the company Chairman, had to make arrangements for a new bank overdraft in 1897. Unfortunately 1898 did not help, because the summer of that year was marred by a long coal strike across South Wales. It ended in September, and traffic recovered gradually, although generally receipts did not approach 1897 levels until the summer of 1899.

As the coal traffic increased, siding space was in short supply. Sandy was strategically situated not only for traffic to the GWR and the Mynydd Mawr stages, but also for traffic to and from the BP&GVR, and a growing number of works nearby. In January 1896, Waddell's asked the L&MMR to approve the provision of new sidings at Sandy estimated at £877 15s. 6d., and the Board agreed that the new sidings 'were a necessity'. In September, and in the following year, the contractor received further 'B' debentures in payment for siding construction.

As business was also growing on the Mansel Lewis line, C.W. Mansel Lewis approached the company about laying a new siding and junction with the L&MMR adjacent to the Old Castle tinplate works. An agreement was sealed on 18th May, 1897, and the connection was duly laid. The newly appointed company Engineer, named Edward Daniel, reported favourably on the junction in October. At the same time he also approved plans for new sidings in Victoria Yard, Llanelly, near the high level line over the GWR. This work was done by the end of the year, but already the Directors felt it was appropriate to ask C.W. Mansel Lewis about the use of more land for sidings at Sandy. In the following October, the Board agreed to erect gates and a gatekeeper's box at the Old Castle crossing, and to build a goods shed and weighbridge at Sandy.

In the second half of the 19th century Llanelly became famous for the manufacture of tinplate, but at this period the industry was experiencing serious difficulties. South Wales was responsible for an astonishingly high proportion of the world's tinplate production until 1891, when the U.S.A. imposed severe tariffs on imported tinplate in order to give American manufacturers a chance to expand. These McKinley tariffs, named after President McKinley, had a dramatic effect upon Llanelly. In some works production had to be suspended for weeks at a time, and tinplate workers soon encountered unaccustomed poverty and unemployment. The Old Castle Iron & Tinplate Co. was the only works with which the L&MMR had a direct connection, but as its iron output was chiefly for use in its own tinplate production, it was as vulnerable as any such works to the changed conditions. From its inception in 1866/7 this company had been managed by the well-respected Joseph Maybery, and following these setbacks he seems to have played a leading role in the formation of a new business to make steel on a site near the Old Castle works.

In January 1897, the Directors found themselves discussing a Parliamentary Bill drafted by the small but increasingly ambitious North Pembrokeshire & Fishguard Railway. This company had been taken over in 1894 by Joseph Rowlands and John Cartland of Birmingham. They were committed to the idea of developing Fishguard as a port for Ireland and North America, and improving access by rail. The NP&F was a most unpromising element in such a vision, being little more than a single and sinuous line across the desolate slopes of the Prescelly hills. The plans before the L&MM Board showed the 'Swansea, Brynamman and Aberdare Extension Railways', an amazing network of new lines curving across South and West Wales liked cooked spaghetti. In this scheme the Mynydd Mawr initially featured as an offshoot of a main line from Carmarthen to the LNWR south of Pontardulais.

Somehow Rowlands must have made it look convincing, because the Directors took it all quite seriously. By February the company and the contractors had agreed to lodge a joint petition against the Bill, and soon after George Blake and George Waddell met with Parliamentary agents in London. On 3rd May, 1897, Mr Stead of Messrs Johnson & Stead, reported to George Blake that Mr Baker, the NP&F's solicitor, had enquired as to whether 'our company would be prepared to entertain a scheme either of amalgamation with the North Pembrokeshire Railway or for a sale to his clients.' Mr Baker had added that the promoters now wished to abandon three of the lines they had previously proposed, and instead hoped 'to utilize the Llanelly and MM Railway as the sole connection with the trunk line and the seaboard which will secure to Llanelly all that can be desired.' However, it was noted that 'an arrangment would be come to with the LNWR for running powers from Pontardulais to Swansea which might of course take some of the traffic from the Cross Hands district to Swansea instead of

Llanelly.' The fact that Mr Stead had had such a meeting was not well received by the L&MM Directors, who resolved that 'all communications between Messrs Baker & Co. and the L&MMR Co. should be through the Secretary of the Llanelly & Mynydd Mawr Company.

As it happened, a new company Secretary by the name of James Morgan had been appointed in April 1897. The NP&F Bill proved to be one of the last occasions that George Blake was active for the L&MM, because he ceased to be Chairman, and a Director in 1898. His replacement was W. Buckley Roderick, who held the chair until his resignation in 1902.

Another objectionable Bill confronted the L&MMR in the very same session of Parliament. This was the Llanelly & Pontardulais Railway (L&PR) Bill. It envisaged the construction of a direct route from the LNWR at Pontardulais, to the harbour at Llanelly, by way of Felin Foel and Furnace. This railway was to join the alignment of the Mynydd Mawr at Sandy, and after throwing off a short branch towards the town centre, it was planned to reach the head of the new North Dock by a bridge over the GWR to the west of the L&MM's high level line. Ironically the Engineer for this project was James B. Walton, who was also Engineer to the NP&FR.

From the L&MMR's point of view this scheme was nothing less than an attempt to confiscate part of its route, and divert traffic over the new line into the North Dock. This feeling was strengthened by the observation that the Harbour Commissioners were assisting the promotion of the project, and that the promoters had shown no interest in negotiating with the company or the contractors. Indeed, George Waddell later referred to the Bill as 'a speculative proposal promoted in reliance of the North Western Company purchasing the powers.' At all events, both the GWR and the L&MMR petitioned against the L&PR Bill, and it was defeated. In the next Parliamentary session, though, the proposal reappeared, and on this occasion the Commissioners had financial assistance from the Llanelly ratepayers to the tune of £1,000. To the satisfaction of the L&MMR, and the frustration of the Commissioners, the Bill again failed.

A less controversial development got under way in 1900. In that year work began on the construction of the second Cwmlliedi reservoir, north of Felin Foel, in the valley sometimes referred to locally as 'Swiss Valley'. The first Cwmlliedi reservoir had been built to provide a new water supply to Llanelly under powers obtained in an Act of 1872. It was formally opened on 17th September, 1878. Powers for the new, upper reservoir were contained in an Act of 1891, and after some delay the construction contract was let to L.P. Nott, who had also been engaged to build the controversial North Dock in Llanelly. On 7th March, 1900, the Mynydd Mawr Board learned of an application from Mr Nott for the provision of a siding adjacent to the new reservoir site. This was agreed on the basis that all expenses would be met by Mr Nott. The siding was duly laid, and it was over 200 ft long with the junction facing north. Located on the west side of the running line, the only access to the reservoir works appears to have been by a cart track. The new Upper Lliedi reservoir was opened formally in July 1903.

In the meantime the L&MMR was considering some plans of its own. One was to revive the old idea of an extension to the LNWR at Llanarthney. The collieries served by both the Mynydd Mawr and the Gwendraeth Valley lines were a considerable distance from markets in all parts of England, and through rates put them at a disadvantage compared with many other coal producers. Welsh geography could not be altered, but rail routes could be improved. The intention of the Llanarthney extension was to reduce the burden of distance and cost for much of the long distance traffic. If this could be done, it was thought that such traffic would increase from 30,000 tons per year from the two lines, to 180,000 tons per year. In addition it was hoped that the extension would stimulate traffic to and from Bancymansel, near Drefach, where both limestone and silica would be worked.

By the autumn of 1900 the civil engineers P.W. & C.S. Meik of Edinburgh were working on the plans and estimates necessary for two proposed lines. No. 1 was to be 7 miles 4 furlongs 2.4 chains long, from the Great Mountain colliery to a junction with the LNWR 257 yards west of Llanarthney station. No. 2 was only 6 furlongs 1.8 chains long, from the BP & GVR at Cwmmawr to a junction with railway No. 1. The engineers estimated the cost of No. 1 to be £82,812, including £9,584 10s. 0d. for tunnelling, and £5,600 for bridges. A modest provision of £1,000 was made for stations. Railway No. 2 was estimated at £7,688, and in the view of the BP & GVR's Engineer, Robert Carr, it involved 'no great engineering difficulties'. He noted, though, that the Mynydd Mawr would have to install gates at the main road crossing at Cwmmawr, whilst exchange sidings would be needed on BP & GV property at the junction just south of Cwmmawr station. He also pointed out that in order to ease some severe gradients the Gwendraeth line would have to be relaid through Pontyberem to Cwmmawr.

Unfortunately, as with so many promising schemes associated with the Mynydd Mawr, this dream failed to materialise. The company borrowed the Parliamentary deposit from the bank in January, and in March their solicitor, James Falconer, wrote to the LNWR's solicitor to report that he had asked the promoters to reconsider the project. 'The fact', he said, 'that your company have made arrangements with the GWR which embrace traffic from the L & MMR and which prevent you from entering into any arrangement with the L & MM seems to them to be so important they do not feel justified in incurring further expense in promoting the Bill at present.' The Bill was dropped, and the idea of the extension died with it.

Although this was a setback for the company and the contractor, Waddell's were never soft in commercial life. Indeed they could be uncompromising in maintaining what they believed to be their rights. In 1902 it appears that the GWR had been making use of the L & MM's junction and track at Old Castle in order to move Llanelly Steelworks traffic, and doing so without reference to either the company or the contractor. Accordingly Waddell's denied the GWR access to the L & MMR for 48 hours from midnight on 5th May, 1902, but advised the Great Western that the L & MM would deliver traffic if asked to do so. Although expert legal opinion was sought on the company's right to charge tolls under their agreements with the GWR and C.W. Mansel Lewis, the problem seems to have been solved without litigation. Waddell's own working agreement with the Mynydd Mawr had expired on 1st January, 1898, but had been renewed regularly thereafter.

Llanelly Harbour Signals

from Llanelly Harbour Commissioners Diagram
Not to Scale

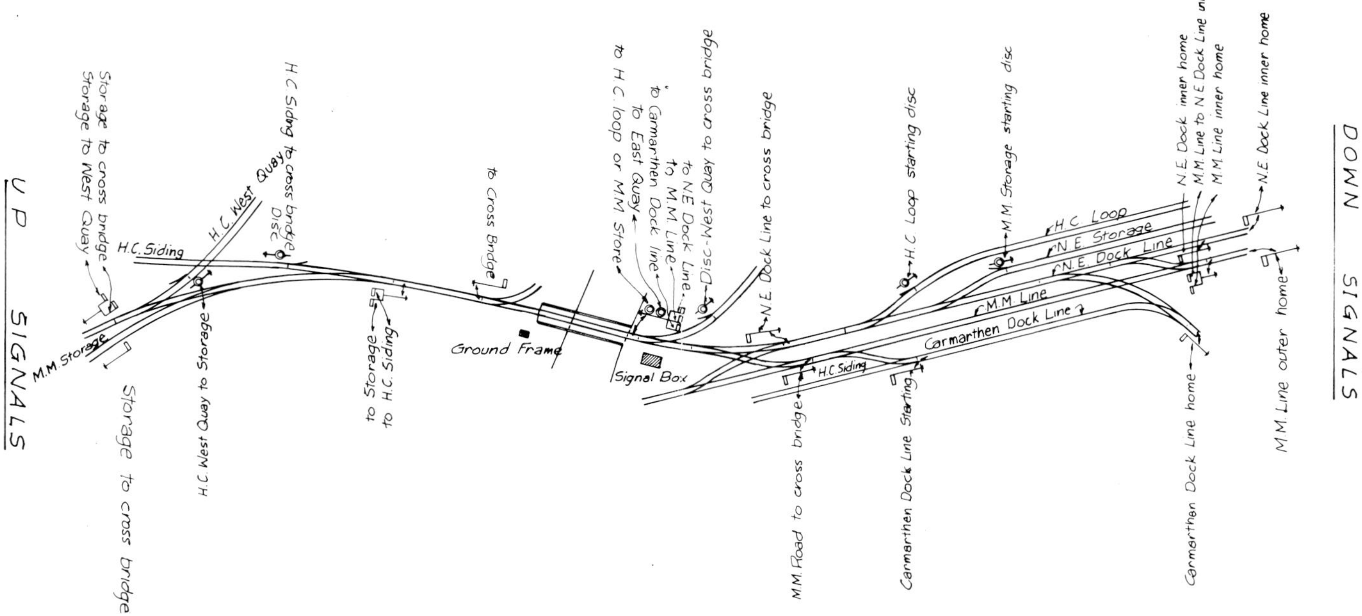

DOWN SIGNALS

UP SIGNALS

M.M Line outer home

N.E Dock Line inner home

M.M Line inner home

M.M Line to N.E Dock Line inner home

N.E Dock inner home

Carmarthen Dock Line home

H.C. Loop

N.E Storage

N.E Dock Line

M.M Line

Carmarthen Dock Line 2

M.M Storage starting disc

H.C Loop starting disc

Carmarthen Dock Line Starting

H.C Siding

M.M Road to cross bridge

N.E Dock Line to cross bridge

Disc–West Quay to cross bridge

to N.E. Dock Line.

to M.M. Line

to Carmarthen Dock line

to East Quay

to H.C. loop or M.M. Store

Signal Box

Ground Frame

to Cross Bridge

to Storage

to H.C. Siding

H.C Siding to cross bridge
Disc

H.C West Quay to Storage

H.C. West Quay

H.C. Siding

Storage to cross bridge

Storage to cross bridge
Storage to West Quay

M.M Storage

NOTE
M.M. – Mynydd Mawr
H.C. – Harbour Commissioners

Harbour Office Llanelly
12. V. 03.

Another idea contemplated at this time was the opening of the railway to passengers under the terms of the Light Railways Act, 1896. The Light Railway Commissioners were consulted about the possibility, but in July 1900, took the view that the curves on the line were too sharp for passenger train safety. Under the 1887 working agreement with the contractor, the company was obliged to find the capital to pay for any improvements. Quite a number were needed. Besides the matter of the track, the line had no signalling, and points were moved only by means of ground levers. In October 1900, Messrs Saxby & Farmer, signalling engineers, produced proposals for signalling the line either to Tumble, or through to Cross Hands colliery, using the 'electric train tablet' system. They suggested that the line should be worked in two or three sections: Llanelly–Cynheidre; Cynheidre –Tumble; and if required Tumble–Cross Hands, on the basis that only one train at a time should be allowed beyond Tumble. Messrs Saxby & Farmer estimated the cost of signalling from Llanelly to Tumble as £861 1s. 7d., and for the entire line as £1344 12s. 1d. At a time when the company faced the expense of litigation over the North Dock dispute, it seems that the sums quoted were sufficient to make the L&MMR defer the matter for 3 or 4 years.

The possibility of passenger traffic may have been a factor in the Directors' decision, in March 1902, to conduct an inspection of the railway, and obtain a report on its condition. If the report was made, a copy has not come to light – but it is clear that numerous improvements were carried out at this period. One of the most interesting was the building of a second locomotive shed, at Victoria Road in Llanelly. On 29th November, 1902, the Directors resolved to provide a corrugated iron shed measuring 45 ft long by 15 ft 6 in. broad, 'in Llanelly station yard'. As the company's papers elsewhere distinguish between Sandy and Llanelly yard, this surely points to Victoria Road as being the intended Llanelly station of the L&MMR. Victoria Road was certainly being developed at this period, as the evidence shows – in 1905, for example, a water column was erected, and in 1906 authority was given for sidings, a weighbridge, coal bins and also a workmen's lavatory. In contrast, at Sandy the chief concern was still to increase siding accommodation – and more was done to this end in 1905 and 1906.

There were also developments outside Llanelly. On 1st March, 1906, the Directors gave their consent to new sidings at Felin Foel and Tumble, and the provision of a cattle loading bank at Cynheidre. They also approved the erection of mileage posts along the line. On 31st March a new private siding agreement was made for the benefit of Great Mountain colliery. Earlier, in December 1903, a similar agreement was sealed with the Caeglas Colliery Co., who were sinking a pit to the east of the railway between Cynheidre and Cwm Blawd.

Further north, the L&MMR and the contractor had negotiated with New Cross Hands Collieries Ltd in 1900 regarding rates for moving coal out from Cross Hands, and for bringing pit timber in from Swansea. An agreement was duly completed on 25th September, 1900. What is less certain is whether any part of Waddell's Norton's branch, to Old Cross Hands colliery, and Gilfach, was still in use. When built it must have made a connection with the GWR's Mountain branch through the colliery sidings. It seems

A ruined engine house at the site of Gorsgoch colliery, viewed across abandoned Mountain branch trackbed; the wooden walled Mountain locomotive shed was very close to this point; 24th March, 1988. *Author*

An early postcard view of Caerbryn Colliery located at the foot of the incline on the Mountain branch from Tirydail to Cross Hands. *R.W. Davies Collection*

A general view of Cross Hands Colliery.   *Author's Collection*

An amazing photograph of Cross Hands miners going underground for an afternoon
shift in 1920.   *Mrs M. Mainwaring*

likely that after the closure of Old Cross Hands colliery in 1887 Waddell's had the use of the railway up to the boundary between the colliery and the GWR. Thereafter it is probable that the GWR did not operate beyond their locomotive shed at Mountain, which was close to Gorsgoch colliery.

A map published in the GWR's own magazine in 1923, depicts Waddell's own extension from Cross Hands to Gilfach. Viewed from Paddington this area was undoubtedly obscure, but by then the extension had been dismantled for many years. The Great Western's Mountain branch alongside it had also been cut back. Although one authority refers to the closure of Mountain shed in 1904, it may well have been abandoned by the GWR much earlier. In the 1890s two other pits above the Mountain branch incline had agreements with the GWR permitting private locomotives to work to the top of the incline. In the case of the Emlyn colliery the agreement was sealed in June 1890, and also covered mileage traffic worked on behalf of the GWR between the incline top and Lamb siding, Penygroes, a point just east of Gilfach, and ¾ mile east of Mountain locomotive shed. After this date, therefore, there was little need for the GWR to keep an engine at Mountain, and it may be supposed that the shed was then closed. On the assumption that after 1890 all traffic above the incline was worked by colliery locomotives, very probably the Mountain branch beyond Lamb siding was itself closed at this time.

By 1902 Waddell's domination of the Mynydd Mawr company was complete. Even the telegraphic address for the company was 'Waddell, Llanelly.' David Kydd became Chairman in 1902, and John Davies, colliery manager of Tumble, joined the Board. David Waddell had been a Director since 1894. In 1904, with the North Dock open, these men felt better able to consolidate the activities of the L & MMR by improving the line and planning for a passenger service. The first step was to re-examine proposals for signalling. In September 1904, Messrs Saxby & Farmer produced estimates for signalling between Sandy Bridge and Tumble, which were virtually identical to the figures quoted four years earlier for the Llanelly–Cross Hands length.

After some delay, the firm of Mackenzie & Holland were consulted. David Kydd then wrote to George Waddell on 15th May, 1906, about a tender for signalling received from Messrs Mackenzie & Holland. He observed that for the sum of £966 1s. 9d. the tender 'includes the minimum of signalling works which they think would be acceptable to the Board of Trade, and the provision of electric staff instruments . . .' Referring to the general condition of the railway, David Kydd said 'things are pretty fair between Llanelly and Tumble, but between Tumble and Cross Hands the work is still unattended to.' As the BP & GV had been contemplating opening to passengers for some time, he ended with a hint of rivalry: 'If we set about our line earnestly the Burry Port might not think it justifiable to open theirs for the same purpose.' This was a vain hope, but at least the L & MMR had now consolidated its position with mineral traffic.

The site of the great dock dispute – Llanelly & Mynydd Mawr stages and embankment in 1899 before the building of the North Dock.
Author's Collection

Chapter Eight
The Great Dock dispute

The immediate result of the opening of the Great Mountain colliery was such an increase in traffic that the construction of a second coal stage was required at Llanelly. It was also proposed that shipping facilities should be improved by the provision of a much enlarged area of layerage by both old and new coal stages. Proposals to this effect were submitted to the Llanelly Harbour Commissioners in May 1889, whereby John Waddell & Sons were to carry out all the works on land (including sidings and sand screens) whilst the works in the harbour were to be done by the Commissioners. On 2nd May, 1889, this arrangement was agreed by the Commissioners at a cost to themselves of £4,000.

At this time the Harbour Commissioners did not own a suitable dredger, and attempted to keep the Carmarthenshire (Mynydd Mawr) berth clear either by the periodic release of water from a large scouring reservoir west of the Carmarthenshire Dock, or by the use of men and shovels. Neither method was very effective, and Waddell's pressed repeatedly for improvements. On 22nd May, 1889, Mr Jennings, the clerk to the Harbour Commissioners requested information about work to be done, stating that 'we have completed an arrangement with the GW Company for the hire of their dredger for 6 weeks.' Whatever was done cannot have been much good because by August 1889, the Commissioners offered to negotiate terms whereby Waddell's would themselves do the work of deepening and levelling the berth at the Mynydd Mawr stages.

Waddell's were willing to assist their own cause in any way, but they still expected the Harbour Commissioners to fulfil their responsibilities. Accordingly on 7th August, 1890, they wrote to Mr Jennings to tell him that they would be starting work in a fortnight on a second coal stage, and to ask that during the two weeks the berth would be closed to coal traffic it 'should be deepened and levelled so that a 1000 tons steamer could lie there with all safety'. They added for good measure 'seeing you have no dredger to carry out this work, we would suggest that it should be done by men excavating and throwing it into the current.' With hindsight such a request seems to have been an exercise in optimism. By February 1891, the Commissioners had returned to John Waddell and Sons to seek their assistance in deepening, straightening and improving the channel. In 1893 the Commissioners' own engineer testified to the effectiveness and permanence of the work carried out.

By then there was a new problem. The two coal stages were located on the eastern side of a long spit of land composed largely of industrial slag and terminating at the harbour light. The sidings serving the stages extended down this embankment, but in 1892 the sea damaged both the embankment and the sidings. Repairs were started but never completed, and in 1895 further damage was caused south of the Mynydd Mawr stages.

In a letter dated 28th November, 1895, Messrs Waddell held the Commissioners responsible for the failure to protect the embankment. They added 'This last slip has shortened our siding room to the extent of another 90 feet which makes it so short that practically it is impossible to ship without our having an engine constantly banking over . . . in addition to the expense of making good the damage, there is this loss being incurred with every ship-ment'.

In spite of other warnings, it appears that the Commissioners did not respond with any urgency. On 12th October, 1896, Waddell's referred to a breach of 25 yards in the embankment, and reported that,

> We have now only siding room beyond our turntables for the storage of trucks . . . on the east line of rails of 15 wagons, and on the west line of rails of 7 wagons, as compared with the former storage capacity of 33 wagons on the east line and 30 wagons on the west line. This curtailment of our storage room involves the constant employment of one of our engines at the tips where shipping is going on instead of as formally our being able to berth an entire cargo in the sidings leaving the engine to do other work.

Not surprisingly, faced with such difficulties in exporting through Llanel-ly, a considerable amount of Mynydd Mawr coal was actually being shipped through Swansea. It was reported that in 1890, 37,000 tons had gone to Swansea, whilst 50,000 tons went through Llanelly. Although total ship-ments were increasing, in the early 1890s the actual proportion going through Llanelly was probably diminishing.

Faced with the reality that Llanelly was losing trade to Swansea and other ports, the Commissioners recognised by 1895 that substantial improvements in their facilities were needed. As a result they went to Parliament in 1896 for powers to construct a new dock (the North Dock) on the site of the existing scouring reservoir. In addition they were empowered to reclaim some land from the Burry Inlet, and to create a new navigable channel from the pier lighthouse to the North Dock. As the embankment of the L&MMR near the Mynydd Mawr stages obstructed the intended entrance to the new dock the Act also included powers for the diversion of the line, and the building of a new portion of the railway across a bridge over the dock entrance.

In 1898 the Commissioners started work on the construction of the North Dock, and before long they found themselves in dispute with John Waddell & Sons. As the new dock was being built on the site of the scouring reservoir, its use had to cease. The Mynydd Mawr stages had benefited by regular scouring but they now began to silt up. As the problem became more serious, the L&MMR had to divert even more of its traffic away to other ports. These problems were not helped by the tide washing out large amounts of material excavated for the new dock.

At an early stage, the Commissioners' contractor correctly applied for and obtained the railway company's consent to lay water pipes and a puddle trench in, or across the railway embankment, but as the work advanced it became necessary to underpin the railway to permit the building of the dock entrance. Having given notice by letter, but without waiting for a reply, the contractor began this work on 9th August, 1899. Mr MacAllister, traffic manager of the L&MMR, intervened to stop him. That evening Mr MacAllis-ter, accompanied by Mr Morgan, the company Secretary, had an 'on site' discussion with Mr Brodie, Engineer of the new dock. There and then the

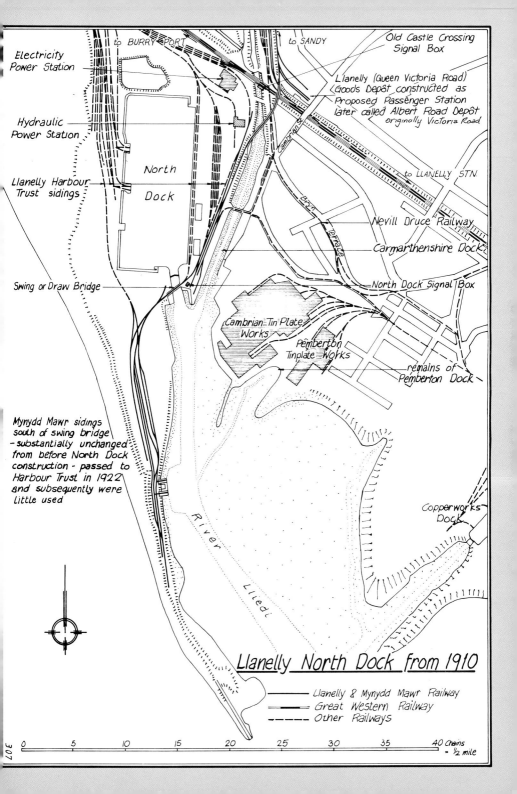

Electricity Power Station

to BURRY PORT

to SANDY

Old Castle Crossing Signal Box

Llanelly (Queen Victoria Road) Goods Depôt constructed as Proposed Passenger Station later called Albert Road Depôt
originally Victoria Road

Hydraulic Power Station

North Dock

to LLANELLY STN.

Llanelly Harbour Trust sidings

Nevill Druce Railway

Carmarthenshire Dock

Swing or Draw Bridge

North Dock Signal Box

Cambrian Tin Plate Works

Pemberton Tinplate Works

remains of Pemberton Dock

Mynydd Mawr sidings south of swing bridge - substantially unchanged from before North Dock construction - passed to Harbour Trust in 1922 and subsequently were little used

River Llied

Copperworks Dock

Llanelly North Dock from 1910

———— Llanelly & Mynydd Mawr Railway
═══════ Great Western Railway
- - - - Other Railways

0   5   10   15   20   25   30   35   40 Chains
= ½ mile

307

contractor's men resumed work, but once again Mr MacAllister intervened. As the workmen continued, Mr MacAllister had some coal wagons shunted onto the track directly above the spot where they were working. To prevent their movement he securely fastened the wheels to the metals with a heavy chain and padlock. Acting on instructions, the workmen responded by smashing the lock releasing the chain. As they returned to their task, Mr MacAllister went up to one of the men and stopped him by holding on to his shovel.

The outcome of this incident was that an undertaking was given on behalf of the contractor that there would be no further interference with the railway without the knowledge of John Waddell & Sons, and the company. However, on Saturday 26th August, the contractor's men returned, removed about 36 feet of ballast and succeeded in underpinning the track. By a remarkable irony, Robert Brodie, the Engineer supervising the works on behalf of L.P. Nott, had worked elsewhere for John Waddell & Sons some years earlier. Although such personal acquaintance might be thought capable of smoothing over differences, there is no evidence that this happened. Indeed, perhaps it is not surprising that Robert Brodie glossed over the whole episode in his published reminiscences.

By now the matter was becoming a source of embarrassment to the local Directors of the L&MMR, W. Buckley Roderick, the Chairman, and Samuel Bevin. In the ensuing row they felt it necessary to distance themselves from the actions of their own contractor, and having noted that they were only consulted after the event, declared no wish to express an opinion 'provided Messrs John Waddell & Sons agree to indemnify the company against all damages, claims, costs, etc. whatsoever'.

The scene was now set for an involved and very protracted dispute. To cut a long story short, the crucial question was whether the land occupied by the L&MMR was held by them by way of easement, or (as the company contended) by way of the Harbour Commissioners lease of 11th January, 1882. The Commissioners assumed that the extent of their grant was an easement; the L&MMR maintained it was a lease, and that they were entitled to a 'notice to treat' in respect of the land. The matter was resolved in the High Court in May 1900, when the railway company obtained an injunction against the Commissioners.

This verdict was a disaster for the Commissioners and the local authority, the Llanelly Borough Council. They were now in the extraordinary position of building a dock without an entrance! The compulsory purchase powers granted by the 1896 Act had expired in 1899, and it was now necessary for the commissioners to promote another Act to revive and extend these powers. In the meantime as the new dock could not be opened they were not receiving additional revenue to meet interest on the large amount they had borrowed. The Llanelly Harbour Act 1901, was duly passed, and the Commissioners borrowed further sums on the same collateral security as before.

If it was hoped that the 1901 Act would rectify difficulties between the Commissioners and the L&MMR, it did not do so. Already there was a history of friction between the two undertakings, and some bitterness on the part of the Waddells. They appear to have received no thanks for their heavy investment in the district, and, indeed, after the Tumble riots of 1893, they and their Scottish staff may well have been regarded as villains. Certainly the Harbour Commissioners did not strive to create a better relationship. In 1898 they aided the promotion in Parliament of the Llanelly and Portardulais Railway, which appeared calculated to threaten the L&MMR.

No doubt frustrated by the failure of this project, and even more by the delays in gaining an entrance to the North Dock, the Commissioners seem to have adopted an increasingly cavalier attitude to the L&MMR and their contractor. They appear to have disregarded continuing complaints about levels at the Mynydd Mawr stages, and in March 1900 they began to operate over a portion of the Mynydd Mawr line at the harbour disregarding payment, or the provision of particulars of the traffic moved. This being a separate issue to that of the dock entrance it was not halted by the injunction obtained by the L&MMR in May 1900.

In the wake of that injunction, and the 1901 Act, further argument arose over the provisions made for the railway company at the harbour. The points at issue were referred to arbitration, and in April 1903 the arbitrator, Peter White, C.E., accepted most of the case made by the L&MMR and John Waddell & Sons. He agreed that the Harbour Commissioners had not kept the company's railway and sidings free from sand and, although they had provided signals for the new swing bridge carrying the railway over the dock entrance, he decided they had not provided the necessary signalling appliances and arrangements to go with them. Accordingly he specified the measures needed, mentioning especially the need for the Commissioners to employ a signalman who would be under the direction of the dockmaster in all matters relating to the swing bridge, and under the direction of the company in all matters relating to the signalling of trains. The arbitrator confirmed that the Commissioners had failed to maintain sufficient access and depth at the berths at the Mynydd Mawr stages, and he also required the Commissioners to improve the provision of moorings.

The parties accepted the arbitration and in December 1903, the North Dock opened for commercial traffic. Under the Llanelly Harbour Act, 1901, the L&MMR were granted rights to ship at the North Dock. Moreover, in July 1903, the Harbour Commissioner offered Waddell a lease of No. 1 hoist at favourable rates, and it appears that from 1904, Messrs Waddell & Sons were shipping their coal at the North Dock. Thereafter the sidings by the Mynydd Mawr stages were used primarily for storage, and (presumably in case of emergency) the stages were retained. Even so, substantial amounts of coal were still sent to Swansea, where the shipping rates were almost certainly cheaper, and where the coal loading facilities were further improved by the opening of the Kings Dock in 1904. At Llanelly, the sense of mutual suspicion was never entirely dispelled, and Messrs Waddell & Sons maintained their claims against the Harbour Commissioners (renamed the Llanelly Harbour Trust in 1904). The Trustees for their part kept a strict record of dock and other dues payable by the railway's contractor, and it seems that neither side would settle accounts until all their differences were resolved.

In 1914, by which time the sums owing amounted to thousands of pounds on both sides, the then Chairman of the Harbour Trust, Sir Stafford Howard

A postcard view of the North Dock, thought to date from the 1920s. Note the Carmarthenshire Dock on the right. *Author's Collection*

Llanelly North Dock, 19th May, 1964. *Michael Hale*

sought a settlement. Progress was being made when the matter was delayed by the outbreak of war. Negotiations resumed after the war and, a settlement was achieved in June 1922, ironically about two weeks before the L&MMR was absorbed by the Great Western Railway. From start to finish the great dock dispute – or disputes – lasted for almost the entire working career of the Llanelly and Mynydd Mawr Railway.

The boarded up signal box and the North Dock entrance seen on 6th November, 1987.
Author

The remains of the Mynydd Mawr stages south of the North Dock entrance, on 6th November, 1987. *Author*

A view looking south at Tumble on 19th August, 1964. The Great Mountain colliery is behind the camera. *Author*

0–6–0PT No. 1643 photographed at the same location on 25th September, 1965, whilst in charge of an RCTS/SLS enthusiasts special train. *H.C. Casserley*

A postcard view of Great Mountain Colliery, Tumble.   *Author's Collection*

Children play and lorries stand idle at the entrance to the site of Great Mountain colliery at Tumble on 5th August, 1990.   *Author*

A wreath laying ceremony when the war memorial at Cross Hands was new. Note the GWR motor bus in the background.

Chapter Nine
The Contractor's Railway

During the nineteenth century there were numerous instances of public railways being worked by contractors. By the 20th century, however, following the absorption of many smaller companies by much larger ones, examples of contractor's railways were becoming rare. Thus the Llanelly & Mynydd Mawr Railway became an outstanding example of a contractor's railway, even though the contractor effectively controlled the company.

This arrangement was interrupted only once in the independent history of the L&MMR. It appears that late in 1907 John Waddell & Sons went into receivership. The reasons for this mishap are not known, but they may have been related to the firm's commitments outside the Llanelly area. At all events, the current working agreement between the company and the contractor expired at the end of 1907, and the contractor's receiver, William Plender, advised the company that he was obliged by court order to cease Waddell's working of the Mynydd Mawr by 31st January, 1908. He proposed that the company should acquire the contractor's rolling stock and plant, subject to the valuation of an arbitrator, Mr W.V. Jull. This was agreed by the Directors on 28th January.

It may be assumed that these steps were taken in the name of the L&MMR, but it seems that in reality George Waddell, as a major shareholder, operated the railway. How much money was actually paid by the company to Plender is not certain, but in February 1909, Plender wrote to the L&MM to say that the court had approved the re-sale to George Waddell of 'all assets, rights, securities, property and effects belonging to the partnership of John Waddell & Sons.' George Waddell accordingly put up £8,086 to allow the company to clear its indebtedness to the receiver, and to enable him to take over all the assets as his own. Although the plant and rolling stock were the property of the L&MMR for almost a year, and in spite of the demise of the original firm of John Waddell & Sons, George Waddell somewhat confusingly traded under the old name. It was as John Waddell & Sons that in January 1909, he offered to work the railway until the end of 1917. His offer was promptly accepted.

Whilst these matters were being resolved, it appears that all improvements to the railway had to wait. In 1909, though, the company and the contractor were ready to move ahead with further works. In April 1909, the Board authorised additions to the new loco shed at Llanelly, including new coal bins and a tool and goods shed. Nearby a handrail was required alongside the track on the section between the high level bridge over the Great Western and the low level junction near Old Castle. Elsewhere many curves on the railway were strengthened by extra sleepering and ballast, and mileposts were erected all along the line. By April 1910, the Directors gave their approval to a sand shed and locomotive water tank at Victoria Road, and also improvements to the older shed at Cille. It was also agreed to make some improvements at Tumble station. At this period the Blaenhirwaun colliery was being opened up to the north of Tumble, and the L&MMR sealed a private siding agreement with the Blaenhirwaun Colliery Co. on 22nd June, 1909.

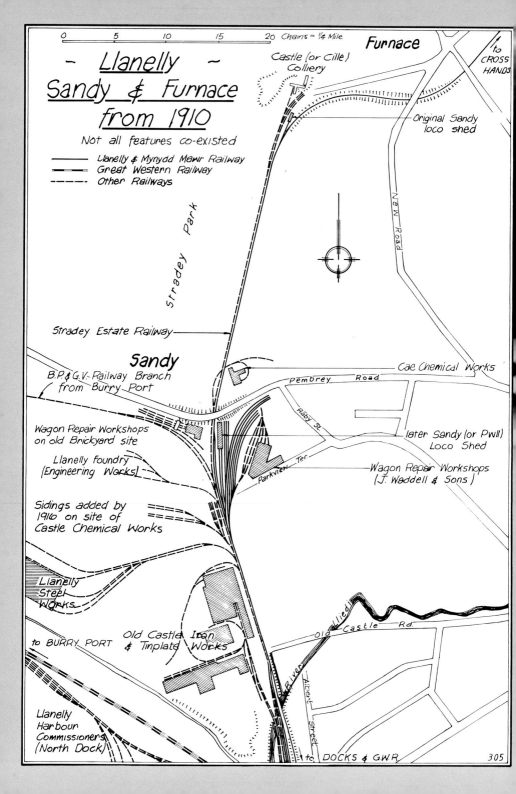

- Llanelly -
Sandy & Furnace
from 1910

Not all features co-existed

——— Llanelly & Mynydd Mawr Railway
═══ Great Western Railway
- - - - Other Railways

Furnace

to CROSS HANDS

Castle (or Cille) Colliery

Original Sandy loco shed

New Road

Stradey Park

Stradey Estate Railway

Sandy

B.P.& G.V. Railway Branch from Burry Port

Cae Chemical Works

Pembrey Road

Raby St.

Wagon Repair Workshops on old Brickyard site

Llanelly foundry (Engineering Works)

Parkview Ter.

later Sandy (or Pwll) Loco Shed

Wagon Repair Workshops (J. Waddell & Sons)

Sidings added by 1916 on site of Castle Chemical Works

Llanelly Steel Works

to BURRY PORT

Old Castle Iron & Tinplate Works

Old Castle Rd.

River

Albert Street

Llanelly Harbour Commissioners (North Dock)

to DOCKS & G.W.R.

305

At Llanelly the local authorities were concerned about the maintenance of the Union road bridge, over the junction of the L&MMR and the GWR, and also of the bridge over the railway at Sandy. As regards the former, an agreement was sealed in January 1907, between the company, the GWR, and the Llanelly UDC, whereby the two railway companies contributed to the cost of maintenance. As regards the more important Sandy bridge, in 1907 and 1908 the County Council sent letters of complaint to the L&MMR, who had earlier undertaken to maintain the road. These objections may have arisen because consideration was then being given to a proposal to construct an electrified street tramway from Llanelly by way of Sandy to Pwll. At any rate, it seems that nothing happened until the tramway contractor's, Balfour Beatty & Co. Ltd, actually carried out work on the Pwll tramway route. This enabled the L&MMR to claim that Balfour Beatty were partially responsible for the poor state of the bridge, and to obtain a contribution from them towards the repairs. Eventually in 1915, the L&MM and the Carmarthenshire County Council entered into a new agreement for the maintenance of the bridge whereby the L&MM contributed £20 annually.

The construction of the electric street tramway in Llanelly must have stimulated fresh thoughts about the desirability of running an official passenger service over the Mynydd Mawr line. Advice was sought from the Board of Trade, and on 16th June, 1911, Colonel Druitt visited the line, having just carried out an inspection of the new street tramway. Accompanied by the young John Waddell, who had succeeded John Davies as a Director in 1909, Col Druitt travelled over the line at least as far as Tumble. The next day he wrote a memorandum on his visit which will be found in Appendix 5. On this and other evidence it seems that he viewed the line as being akin to a light railway, and adequate for passenger working provided numerous modifications and improvements were made.

The company made no immediate response, but maintained its policy of making gradual improvements, and quietly operated a workmen's service over the whole length of the line north from Sandy. Inevitably the running of this service became known to other inhabitants of the district, and in December 1912 Mr D.M. Jenkins wrote to the Board of Trade to ask if the L&MMR could be compelled to run a public passenger service, as authorised in the Acts of 1875 and 1880. Initially the Board of Trade was non committal, but in January 1915, Mr Jenkins, writing on behalf of the Cross Hands Improvement Co., raised the question again. Pointing out that the L&MMR ran colliers' trains every weekday between Llanelly and Cross Hands, he added that 'a charge is made for every collier carried.' The Board of Trade now declared their belief that the company could not be compelled to run a public passenger service, but chose not to investigate the service of dubious legality that had been reported to them. This omission may well have arisen from special circumstances of wartime, and yet even in 1919 the Board of Trade noted that the service was being operated, and that no action was being taken upon it.

Returning to 1911, many working people were then experiencing a decline in their standard of living, and industrial unrest was widespread. In August 1911, the first ever national rail strike became the occasion of one of

After the shooting of August 1911 – a GWR train halted by the disturbance on the
main line adjacent to the junction with the L & MMR.   *Llanelli Public Library*

Aftermath of the riot at Llanelly GWR Goods Yard, 1911 (note the Cross Hands
private owners wagons).   *Llanelli Public Library*

the unhappiest events in the history of Llanelly. The background and the detail of this occurrence have been described admirably by John Edwards in 'Remembrance of a Riot'. Suffice to say that the strikers in Llanelly directed their attention primarily on the obstruction of the GWR main line, and virtually ignored the L&MMR. However, on 19th August, a crowd which gathered near the junction of the L&MM and the Great Western began stoning a train which was receiving the protection of troops. The Riot Act was read, apparently unheard by many of those present, and as the crowd failed to disperse the troops fired five shots. Two men were killed and two others injured. In the ugly atmosphere which then developed there were further disturbances in the town, and an explosion in the GWR goods yard which caused four more fatalities. By then, ironically, the strike had just been settled. Railway operations soon returned to normal, but this occasion caused considerable shock to the good people of Llanelly, and a sense of shame which endured for years afterwards.

From 1911 or 1912 it seems that the company became concerned about the handling of traffic between the GWR and the Llanelly steelworks. The proximity of the junction with the GWR to the connection with the Mansel Lewis private railway, and to the steelworks itself, evidently contributed to the idea that some traffic was being worked over Mynydd Mawr rails by the GWR, to the detriment of the company. Accordingly a man was given the job of watching and recording steelworks traffic, to ensure that the company could claim its proper share of the charges arising. Thereafter the appropriate figures were noted annually in the company minutes.

If the GWR was ever tempted to use L&MMR rails to its own advantage, the latter itself was not above suspicion of behaving in a similar way. On 17th May, 1913, Mr C.R. Mansel Lewis wrote to the company with the allegation that 'you have recently been hauling trucks of materials for some party over our line to Cille.' On 2nd June he wrote again, noting the movement of three trucks of slates and bricks for Phillips of Furnace. On both occasions he wished to know the precise identity of the assignee, so that he might be charged for the traffic passed. The available notes suggest that the L&MM may have continued to work over the private railway until 21st August, although some of their activities may have been authorised. At all events, the argument rumbled on in to the autumn, with Mr Mansel Lewis clearly unhappy at the company's interpretation of the 1897 agreement on the working of traffic.

In the years before World War I the Great Western invested heavily in developing facilities at the Pembrokeshire port of Fishguard, hoping to see it attract transatlantic as well as Irish traffic. Part of the GWR's expenditure was directed towards improving the railway connections to Fishguard, and in 1913 a Bill was prepared seeking powers for a new line avoiding Llanelly and its many junctions and crossings. The proposed line was intended to run north of the town, via Furnace and Stradey Park to Pembrey, crossing the L&MMR. However, this scheme was abandoned with the onset of war, and the only line improvement completed was the Swansea District line, avoiding Swansea.

Pursuing their policy of making gradual improvements, the Directors continued to approve works for the benefit of the railway in general, and the possibility of a public passenger service in particular. In February 1912, they accepted Waddell's offer to lay more sidings at Sandy at a cost of £1,000, and in the next month they authorised the erection of a new weighbridge at Sandy, and additional improvements at Tumble station. On 17th February, 1913, the company and the contractor sealed an agreement with the recently formed New Cross Hands Collieries Ltd for the latter's use of L&MMR track and Waddell's land at Cross Hands. Shortly after, perhaps in anticipation of colliery developments, it was decided to buy land for sidings at Cynheidre. By 1914 work done or proposed included the strengthening of numerous curves by the addition of sleepers, and the realignment of an especially sharp curve at Quarry Mawr. The junction with the GWR was being relayed, and another siding provided adjoining Albert Street in the nearby Victoria Road yard. A water tank and new drains were installed at Tumble, and by 1915 improvements at Old Castle were also in hand.

The improvements made to the Mynydd Mawr line indicate that the company's financial position was becoming stronger. Outside Llanelly the L&MMR now served collieries at Cross Hands, Blaenhirwaun, Great Mountain, Caeglas and Mynydd Sylen. Near to the last mentioned pit at Horeb, the Blackthorn Brickworks Co. had opened their works in 1907; it became better known as the Eclipse, or Horeb, brickworks. Traffic was increasing, and the coming of World War I ensured that the railway remained busy. In 1915 the main need was for more sidings; towards the end of the year the contractor produced accounts for sidings comprising 92½ yds at Tumble, 599 yds at Cynheidre, and 757½ yds at Sandy. In the following year another 122½ yds of sidings were installed at Cynheidre, and at Llanelly a new cabin was constructed and the locomotive shed re-roofed. In 1917 siding accommodation was provided at Victoria Road yard for the repair of wagons, and the telephone was installed. Minor works were also carried out nearby at Mansfield House, as well as at Cwmblawd, Tumble and Cross Hands. A water tank was added at Brondini (Cynheidre) and a further siding laid at Sandy.

The available records offer regrettably little information about this interesting period on the railway. The siding construction at Sandy is a pointer to the extent to which this spot had become the marshalling yard for L&MMR traffic to the GWR, the BP&GVR, and the docks. At about this time it is thought that Waddell's built their own wagon works at Sandy, close to the site of Alexander Raby's forge. Almost certainly they were also responsible for building a new two road locomotive shed for the L&MMR, on the east of the line, just south of the bridge at Sandy. As no progress had been made with the development of a passenger station at Victoria Road, and the emphasis was entirely upon freight traffic, this was a logical step. However, no specific mention of a locomotive shed at Sandy appears in the company's papers before December 1917, when there is a reference to a payment of £23 4s. 9d. in respect of it. As the shed measured 130 ft by 30 ft, and was solidly built in brick with a slate roof, it was not cheap to construct. Accordingly it must be supposed that it was paid for by the contractor, and completed in 1917 or 1918. As no more is heard thereafter of an engine shed at Llanelly, as

Victoria Road was often described, it must be assumed that not long after that shed was closed.

Whatever the truth about this matter, the provision of a wagon works seems to have been a shrewd move on the part of Waddell's. Under wartime conditions wagons were worked hard, and given relatively little mainte-nance. After the war the L&MMR had to make some sizeable payments to both Great Mountain colliery and to Blaenhirwaun colliery in respect of damage to wagons. The latter was now controlled by S&R Anthracite Col-lieries Ltd.

Throughout the war L&MMR Board meetings usually comprised the Chairman, David Kydd, and John Waddell, with James Morgan, the com-pany Secretary in attendance. Although David Waddell remained a Director, he now had an address at Blackhall, Midlothian. A brother-in-law, E. Robertson Grant, joined the Board in 1914, but was also almost invariably absent. In the autumn of 1917 this small directorate decided to seek tenders for working traffic on the railway for five years from 1st January, 1918. To no one's surprise, the only tender came from John Waddell & Sons, offering to renew the existing agreement for a further 10 years. This was soon accepted.

At the beginning of the war all railway companies had been placed under governmental control. The most notable consequences were the introduc-tion of the eight hour day for all grades of railwaymen, and a movement towards the standardisation of wage rates throughout the country. These changes certainly helped to keep vital wartime traffic on the move, but they also brought about a dramatic increase in operating expenses. John Waddell & Sons felt these effects keenly. On 6th February, 1919, a letter from the contractor was placed before the Board. The firm wrote: 'Under the excep-tional circumstances of the excessive wages and costs we cannot continue to run the railway at our expense from 31st December, 1918, and can only agree to carry on until other arrangements are made, and on your undertaking to free and relieve us of all loss and expense in the matter from 31st December, 1918.' The L&MM Directors felt that they had no option but to give the undertaking, pending any other arrangements.

The L&MMR was quite possibly the only public railway ever to have held Board meetings in England (1880), Wales and Scotland. The next meeting took place on 11th October, 1919, at 21 St. Andrew's Square, Edinburgh, at Waddell's offices. John Waddell and E. Robertson Grant were present, together with Thomas Arnott, standing in for James Morgan. Strangely no direct reference was made to the issue raised in the previous February, or to the sudden death on 18th March of George Waddell. By this time he had been given the title 'General Manager', and after some delay this title was bestowed upon John Waddell, together with an initial salary of £500 a year. John Waddell's place on the Board was taken by George Crawford of Edin-burgh.

The problem of increased operating costs was so widespread that, in 1919, it was decided that governmental control of the railways should continue for a further two years whilst future policy was discussed. Before long it was concluded that if the larger railways absorbed the smaller companies, the burden of running costs would be spread out more fairly between the rich

The only official public passenger service on rails from Llanelly to Felin Foel!
R.W. Davies Collection

A scene on the opening day of the Llanelly & District Electric Traction Co. service in July, 1911.
R.W. Davies Collection

and the poor. Whilst legislation for the 'grouping' of companies was being prepared, the L&MMR and Waddell's sought to reach an agreement of their own. On 9th April, 1920, the Directors agreed to take over the plant and rolling stock of John Waddell & Sons as at 31st December, 1918, at a valuation of £16,746. A depreciation fund was started to meet this expense, on the understanding that the plant and stock would remain the contractor's property until they were fully paid. A further £9,172 9s. 7d. was outstanding in favour of Waddell's under their principal agreement, and in relation to other expenditure incurred.

By 1920 the prospect of the GWR taking over the Mynydd Mawr may have encouraged some fresh thinking about the possibility of a public passenger service from Llanelly. At all events the Great Western railmotor No. 75, carried out clearance trials over the line. Unfortunately the dream of an official passenger service still proved to be elusive, although a busy workmens' service from Sandy to Cross Hands continued to function, subject to government directions as to the fares payable.

Some people managed to travel on the line quite illegally, as was revealed in a letter from the company to the police at Tumble in 1922. This dispatch pointed out that certain residents of the village were entering empty coal wagons at Tumble, and in some cases walking a mile down the line and riding up on the axle boxes. More seriously, though, it reported that points at Tumble had been tampered with, diverting an afternoon coal train from Cross Hands into the siding at Tumble station, causing considerable damage.

Earlier, in July 1920, James Morgan retired through ill health, and it was agreed that the experienced company Chairman, David Kydd, should take over the post of company Secretary. He was succeeded as a Director by Thomas Arnott, and as Chairman by George Crawford. By now there was little left for the company to do, but to try to tidy up its affairs. The most important issue was the final settlement of the great dock dispute. Having reached a provisional agreement with the Harbour Trust in 1914, further delays ensued, and the matter was not dealt with until 1922. The Harbour Trust then agreed to pay the contractor and the company £16,000, on the basis that they would surrender the rights they had held under the 1882 lease. The effect of the agreement was to put the L&MMR on the same footing as every other trader using the North Dock.

John Waddell, as General Manager, played an important part in these negotiations, and also in the negotiations with the GWR prior to the 'grouping' taking effect. The railway was no longer a 'lame duck', desperately in need of support; the GWR was acquiring a line which had witnessed an astonishing growth in business during the first two decades of the century, and now employed almost 100 people. Quite reasonably on its absorption into the Great Western in 1922 the L&MMR was allowed to pay a dividend of 6% on ordinary share capital of £59,300. The company was also allowed to retain £4,250 received from the government under the Railways Act, 1921, to satisfy claims for loss of office by John Waddell, David Kydd and the Engineer Mr Macallister. The GWR, however, resisted an attempt by these officers to claim privilege tickets and annual passes on the grounds that there was no existing agreement for the exchange of such benefits.

Pannier tanks Nos. 1607 and 1618 in the sidings above Great Mountain colliery on
3rd June, 1953.   *R.C. Riley*

0–6–0PT No. 1607 on the L&MM line at Great Mountain on 3rd June, 1953.
                                                                         R.C. Riley

Cross Hands Colliery sidings, 3rd June, 1953 showing the sad state of the trackwork.
R.C. Riley

Pannier tank No. 1607 takes a rest between shunting movements at Cross Hands colliery on 3rd June, 1953.
R.C. Riley

At a Special General Meeting of shareholders held in Llanelly on 8th December, 1922, the Chairman referred to 'the indebtedness of the proprietors to Mr Waddell for the great ability he had displayed in conducting the negotiations and the satisfactory terms he had arranged for the proprietors.' Although as controlling shareholders the Waddells had the most to gain, it was fitting for one of the family to receive such a tribute. Throughout the entire operating career of the L&MMR the Waddells had managed and maintained the railway. Even if the distinction between the public railway company and their contractor was quite marginal, the Mynydd Mawr was still a contractor's line, and arguably the finest example of its kind. On 1st January, 1923, 40 years to the day after the official opening of the line, the Great Western assumed control, and brought down the curtain on the Llanelly & Mynydd Mawr Railway and its contractor's operations.

A study of desolation and remarkable trackwork at Cross Hands at the top of the Llanelly and Mynydd Mawr Railway, on 19th August, 1966.   *Author*

Chapter Ten
L&MMR Rolling Stock and Rail Services

PASSENGER STOCK AND SERVICES

The story of the L&MM's passenger service is one of the most interesting, and yet elusive, aspects of the line's long history. When the Great Mountain colliery was opened in 1887 the population on Mynydd Mawr was extremely sparse, and it may well be supposed that from the outset some colliers were conveyed to and from the pit in the contractor's diminutive wagons or brakevans. At present there is no evidence for or against the operation of workmen's trains in the 19th century, although there is a strong local tradition that in the early days of the line a person wishing to travel over the route would be allowed to ride with the guard. Indeed, it is said that anyone wishing to make a brief visit to Llanelly could travel down with the morning coal train, and return in the afternoon with the empty wagons.

By 1900 the L&MMR was keenly interested in running a public passenger service and, as has been noted, discussed the possibility with the Light Railway Commissioners. Although the cost of their recommendations appears to have deterred the company from acting upon them, it seems very probable that John Waddell & Sons operated their own unofficial service at this period. Not surprisingly, perhaps, there are no proper records to be found, and reminiscences must suffice. In 1989 a lady of 100 recalled how, even in 1903, a young woman from the Pontyberem area travelled daily to work in Llanelly by way of the Mynydd Mawr line. At this date, it is said, the passengers travelled either in the guard's van, or in colliers' vans which had an open doorway at the centre on both sides and seating around the van walls inside. These trains ran to and from the bridge at Sandy.

According to William Timbrell's *Memoirs of Tumble from 1896*, the L&MMR operated a Saturday afternoon passenger service with a train comprising 'three or four long coaches with seats along the full length on each side, which were ideal for shopping expeditions.' Unfortunately no dates are given for either the start or the finish of this particular service. The author simply states that the service was 'very popular and well patronised', but was discontinued after some time to the dismay of the villagers who used it. The only explanation offered was that local tradesmen had objected, owing to their loss of trade. The author appears to say that the coaches were last used 'to take Reservists and Territorials to war in 1914.'

The description of these coaches does not match that of any of the others known to have worked over the line, and thus gives rise to the view that William Timbrell has provided an account of the earliest railway coaches to be used on the L&MMR. However, whilst it must be assumed that the trains were operated by John Waddell & Sons, it is not at all clear whether the contractor bought or borrowed or hired the rolling stock. There is simply no reference to such a train in the records of the L&MMR.

Speculation on the subject may be hazardous, but it seems possible that the contractor may have made an arrangement to borrow or hire stock from the BP&GVR for this market day service. In 1899 two collieries in the Gwendraeth valley, at Pont Henry and Pontyberem, acquired a pair of bogie

By 1922 the condition of much of the L&MMR was so poor that the GWR elected to move it to Swindon on other wagons, although these L&Y wagons may also have belonged to the L&MMR.   *British Rail*

coaches from the Ashbury Railway Carriage Co. These vehicles were 46 ft
2 in. long, with seating running lengthwise down the coaches, and two
doors at each end. Although used primarily for colliers, it is known that at
this period a one coach train was run on Thursdays 'to carry colliery women
to and from market'. As the market was actually in Llanelly, this service
must have worked to Sandy via Pwll. Suffice to say that the use of these
coaches on the L&MM on Saturdays (and perhaps also Thursdays) appears
to be within the bounds of possibility.

On 6th September, 1903, there was a fatal accident on the BP&GVR near
Burry Port when a light engine collided with a workmen's train. At the
ensuing enquiry, officers of the Board of Trade were astounded to learn that
some of the passengers were colliers' wives. Furthermore it emerged that the
company had no authority to carry passengers in brakevans and wagons, and
that the market day trains were entirely illegal! In spite of Board of Trade
criticism, the BP&GVR seems to have continued these services, allowing
market day passengers to travel free, apart from a charge of 6d. per item of
luggage. Nevertheless, the 1903 accident was clearly a warning to both the
BP&GV and the L&MM to put their passenger operations on a proper
footing. By February 1904, the BP&GV was discussing its arrangements with
the Board of Trade, whilst later that same year the Directors of the L&MM
were taking a fresh look at Messrs Saxby & Farmer's proposals for signalling
between Sandy and Tumble.

On 5th June 1905, the L&MM Secretary, James Morgan, wrote to the Board
of Trade saying 'the company are in some doubt by reason of the habits of
the local population generally whether a daily service would yield them a
satisfactory return.' He then asked, somewhat tongue in cheek, if the Board
of Trade would issue a certificate for the company to 'run passenger trains
intermittently as they may deem necessary.' By this James Morgan hoped to
win consent for public passenger services on Thursdays and Saturdays, the
two Llanelly market days. However the Board of Trade replied by referring
the company to the Regulation of Railways Act, 1842.

Although the L&MM made numerous improvements to its facilities, it
seems to have hesitated to spend the money necessary to improve the track
and install signalling. Possibly this was linked to the financial difficulties
experienced by the contractor in 1907 and 1908. At all events, whilst the
L&MMR maintained its workmen's service, the BP&GVR set about the
reconstruction of its main line from Burry Port to Pontyberem to bring it up
to the standard required for public passenger traffic. The consulting engineer for this work was none other than the famous light railway specialist,
H.F. Stephens. The BP&GVR officially opened for passengers to Pontyberem
on 2nd August, 1909, and to Cwmmawr on 29th January, 1913.

Reminiscences do not necessarily provide the most reliable guide to the
past, but in the case of the Mynydd Mawr line need to be noted. Hence there
is reason to believe that coaches as well as colliers' vans were in use in the
Edwardian period. The origin of the coaches described by William Timbrell
cannot be determined with certainty. In addition it seems that some 4-wheel
compartment stock appeared on the railway, but speculation that this may
have come from the Mersey Railway (with which Waddell's had been close-

The L&MM coach bodies were lifted from their underframes before despatch to Swindon. No. 6 was a former Metropolitan Railway 3rd class coach. *British Rail*

Van bodies received similar treatment as stated above. *British Rail*

ly associated) is not yet supported by any documentary evidence. What is clear, though, is that by 1911 the workmen's service was sufficiently well established for Edmondson card tickets to be issued to the passengers.

In 1913 John Waddell & Sons acquired eight second-hand 'Jubilee' type 4-wheel carriages from the Metropolitan Railway. Six of these were third class, having five compartments each, and the other two were brake thirds with three compartments each. An additional brake third, numbered either 9 or 9A, appears to have been purchased by the contractor at about the same time, and is thought to have come from the Metropolitan Railway via the Bute Works Supply Co. of Cardiff. All these carriages are believed to have had 'Carriage No. x' painted in full on the carriage waist, to avoid any confusion with the compartment numbers painted on the door panels. This stock was originally lit by acetylene gas lamps, and on the L&MMR ran without the benefit of any kind of continuous brake. Although these carriages saw regular use through World War I, they were almost always stabled in the open, and so deteriorated rapidly. By 1921 they are believed to have been dumped out of use in sidings at Sandy. In 1923 they were found to be unfit to travel on their own wheels, so the bodies were detached from their underframes and the remains were transported to Swindon on GWR bogie wagons. It would surely have been easier to scrap them at Llanelly.

In January 1920, the question of running a public passenger service over the railway was raised once again, and it was suggested that such a service might be provided economically by giving the Great Western running powers for the purpose. The GWR did not care for the proposal, but offered to lend one or two railmotor cars to the L&MMR to enable it to operate such a service. In May 1920, with the encouragement of the Ministry of Transport, railmotor No. 75 was dispatched to Llanelly to run clearance trials over the L&MMR. By August the Ministry had reviewed the overall situation, but had come up with the familiar view that bringing the line up to the standard required for a regular passenger service would be prohibitively expensive. Once again the idea was dropped.

On Mondays, Tuesdays and Wednesdays the chief cashier, Henry Griffiths, travelled on the workmen's train, and at Cynheidre he and another employee based at Tumble would collect fares from the men working at Blaenhirwaun and Cross Hands collieries. As the L&MM was so closely associated with the Great Mountain colliery the fares of the Tumble miners were deducted through their pay packets, although after the GWR took control of the railway it seems that the Tumble men paid on the train like everyone else. In 1921 a lady clerk at Great Mountain regularly took the train from Horeb to Tumble, and was treated with courtesy by the colliers.

In 1990 William Davies of Cefneithin, Cross Hands, gave the writer a fascinating glimpse of the workmen's service in the early 1920s when he was employed at Great Mountain. The train was known to the workmen as 'the Spake', a term normally associated locally with the small and somewhat primitive rail transport which took colliers down into mine drifts or levels. On the Mynydd Mawr line at this period 'the Spake' usually comprised only coaches, but on occasions it is said to have been a double-headed mixed train, with empty wagons behind the locomotives and up to nine or ten

Two views of condemned L & MMR stock on arrival at Swindon Works.

coaches at the rear, assisted as necessary by a banking engine. The coaches were old and decrepit, with bare wooden seats and no lights. The windows had no glass, and only sacking for cover. Small platforms were provided at Furnace and Felin Foel, and according to another report there may have been a short, low platform at Cwm Blawd also. All the stopping places were dignified with the title of 'station', but the small halt at Dynant, between Cwm Blawd and Tumble, appears to have been abandoned by or during World War I. At Cross Hands the terminus was known simply as 'station fach', and the coaches were kept in sidings nearby whilst not in use.

The colliers' shift at Great Mountain ended at 3.00 pm, and as there were no pithead baths at the colliery until about 1935, the men gathered at the station soon after. Their comfort and convenience being secondary to the shunting of wagons at Cross Hands, they regularly had to wait some time in the open for the train home – frequently half an hour, and sometimes longer. In wet or wintery conditions this was no joke! As a result the colliers were rarely back home before 6.00 pm, and were often later, and in winter never had any daylight to enjoy. The men who lived or lodged in colliery company property at Tumble had some compensations!

According to one authority, the late Eric Mountford, the Mynydd Mawr workmen's service reverted to colliers' vans after the L&MM coaches had been abandoned. The recollections of a few local people suggest that coaches and colliers' vans were still to be seen. It is just possible that the contractor may have hired some elderly 4-wheel coaches from the GWR before 1923; there is evidence that Great Western stock was employed after 1923. In 1989 a former employee of the L&MMR, Harry Brown, remembered an occasion in the 1920s when a replacement door was sent down from Swindon for one of the coaches in use on the line.

> The passenger train had gone up at 5.30 am, taking the miners to work. The missing door had been covered with a piece of sacking, we followed up on the 6.00 am goods train, and put on that new door. It had a '3' painted on it, for third class. None of the other Mynydd Mawr coaches had markings on them then. When the miners came back to the train every single one of them opened that door to see what was behind it!

The rolling stock described may have come from the Neath & Brecon Railway, where the carriages on the workmen's trains carried no markings. However, by 1927 only five N&BR carriages were still in GWR stock.

It has been suggested to the writer that about 400 miners a day used the Mynydd Mawr workmen's service, implying that in a six day week up to 2,400 return journeys would be recorded. In 1920 no less than 136,000 passenger journeys were made on the L&MMR – a remarkable figure for a line without authority to run advertised passenger trains, and an indication that a sizeable number of journeys were being made by people other than miners. It is all the more remarkable when it is remembered that the GWR had started a motor bus service between Llanelly and Cross Hands by about March 1913, and that other local bus operators set up business soon after. Indeed, in the 1920s the need for a workmen's service diminished as bus services improved, although the GWR went to the trouble of printing its own tickets for the service between Sandy and Cross Hands. It is believed that use of the trains declined sharply after the 1926 General Strike, and eventually ended in 1929, or 1930.

FREIGHT STOCK AND SERVICES

Very little is known of freight services in the L&MM's earliest days. The figures recorded for train miles worked before 1887 are pitifully low. In the first six months to the end of June 1883, only 3,822 miles were worked, indicating perhaps one trip from Llanelly to Cross Hands and back each day, five days per week. By the equivalent period of 1884 the total was even worse – merely 1,872 train miles worked. Although the figures improved to 5,400 miles in the second half of 1884, the total fell back to 1,872 miles in the second half of 1885. By then both Gilfach and Gorsgoch collieries had closed, and it may be supposed that the old Cross Hands (Norton's) colliery was struggling vainly to stay in business.

Two years later the situation was transformed by the opening of the Great Mountain Colliery. In the half year ending in December 1887, some 11,467 train miles were worked, and in the same period of 1888 the total reached 15,290 miles. This figure implies up to four return trips being made over the railway each day; traffic tonnage in 1888 is believed to have been in excess of 50,000. Some caution must be expressed about the train miles figures, though, because for several years thereafter the December total was customarily given as 15,290, and sometimes the June figure as its half, 7,645. It would seem that these numbers had become convenient estimates for a freight service which probably comprised only two return journeys over the whole line on each working day.

Three, or even four, return trips daily may have been achieved up to December, 1897, when 24,700 train miles were worked. In the half year to December, 1898, however, at a period of industrial unrest, the figure dropped to 7,720 miles only. A total of 25,000 train miles worked was reached for the first time in the half year to December 1900. The year 1900 is believed to have been the first in which over 100,000 tons were carried on the L&MMR. By 1920 some 417,000 tons were moved over the line, 364,000 tons being coal.

Unfortunately no working timetables for the L&MMR have come to light, but the earliest GWR timetable available (1927) is thought to reflect the pattern of services on the railway after World War I. This timetable is reproduced on pages 128 and 129; the two return workings between Sandy and Cynheidre were probably for the benefit of the Llanon Valley Anthracite Colliery Co., established at Cynheidre in 1922. As might be expected the timetable shows all services terminating at Sandy, and appears to suggest that all traffic to and from the Mynydd Mawr line travelled by way of Old Castle Junction. No reference is made to the L&MM's route to the docks over the South Wales main line, or to the coal and goods depot at Victoria Road (later Queen Victoria Road), although the latter was in use.

Nothing is known of the original rolling stock provided by John Waddell & Sons, but in view of the decayed condition of much of the stock in 1923 it seems possible that some vehicles may have lasted for most of the independent existence of the railway. When the L&MMR was absorbed on 1st

January, 1923, it had a dismal collection of wagons and vans to hand over to the GWR. The figures for L&MM open wagons at this date is given variously as 24 or 26, with either 11 or 12 covered vans or wagons. There were also three small brakevans, each weighing a mere 6 tons. The Great Western authorities soon decided that most of these vehicles were not fit to travel to Swindon on their own wheels, and had them loaded on to other wagons. The photographs taken of this stock at Swindon before scrapping not only reveal the extent of their decay, but also that they were generally fitted with dumb buffers. The private owner wagons used by the colliery companies along the line were almost certainly of better quality, because they had to work over the GWR as well as the L&MMR. Those belonging to Great Mountain, Blaenhirwaun and New Cross Hands collieries were all painted black with white lettering.

LOCOMOTIVES

An excellent history of L&MMR locomotives was published in Part 10 of *The Locomotives of the GWR, 1922–1947*, published by the Railway Corres-pondence and Travel Society in 1966. That account has never been seriously criticised, and rather than cover the same ground in such considerable detail, this description of the locomotives will focus on the main points of interest and any details previously unpublished.

The first engine to work on the railway, at the start of construction in April 1880, was the contractor's locomotive *The Baron*. Unfortunately the only available reference to this machine comes in a contemporary press report, and further details are not available. However, it was very probably a small tank locomotive somewhat similar to the Andrew Barclay locomotive (works number 219) delivered new to Waddell's at Llanelly in October 1880. By 1885 it had been transferred to colliery proprietors named Bowman & Co., of Buckhaven, Fife, and it later passed to the Wemyss Coal Co. who withdrew it for scrap in 1928.

Another Andrew Barclay locomotive (works number 221 of 1880) was delivered new to the railway, reportedly in the month of November 1881, about a year after construction. If the date of delivery is correct, it must be assumed that the honour of hauling the first trains on the L&MMR fell to Andrew Barclay 219, although as an 0–6–0 saddle tank engine No. 221 was probably better able to deal with the gradients on the line. At all events, this locomotive was named *John Waddell*, and it worked on the L&MMR for many years. After being rebuilt by the Avonside Engine Co. of Bristol in 1901/2, it eventually went into colliery service in Lancashire in about 1908. Then named *Astley Green*, after the pit where it was employed, it was sold for scrap in May 1936, by Manchester Collieries Ltd.

At this period there seems to have been a significant association between John Waddell and the Scottish locomotive builders, Andrew Barclay & Sons. In 1882 the latter were in some financial difficulty, and received sufficient assistance from John Waddell, and a certain Thomas Steven, to be able to continue trading. One other Andrew Barclay product came to the L&MMR, namely *Inveravon* (works number 199 of 1879) in about September 1887, from Messrs Scott & Best, contractors of Leith. Its career was extremely brief,

An early locomotive on the L & MMR – Andrew Barclay 221.   *F. Jones Collection*

A later Barclay 0 – 6 – 0ST – *E.J. Roberton Grant.*   *F. Jones Collection*

Merkland of the L & MMR climbs away from Furnace (assisted by a banking engine) with a train of empty wagons.   *LCGB Ken Nunn Collection*

The Hudswell, Clarke 0–6–0ST *John Waddell* at Great Mountain colliery, Tumble, in 1948.   *F. Jones*

Table One

JOHN WADDELL & SONS' LOCOMOTIVES

Contractor for construction of Llanelly & Mynydd Mawr Railway; also provided rolling stock and worked the traffic. Line opened 1st January, 1883. Absorbed by GWR 1st January, 1923.

Name	Type	Builder	Maker's No.	Built	Cyls	Driving Wheels	Remarks
John Waddell	0-4-0ST OC	AB	219	1880	12 × 20	3' 6"	New to Llanelly 10/1880 to Bowman & Co.. (colliery proprs.) Buckhaven, Fife, 1885.
	0-6-0ST OC Reb	AB AE	221	1880 1901/2	14 × 20 Later quoted as 14 × 21	3' 6" 3' 9"	New to Llanelly 11/1881. Sold 1908 to Clifton & Kersley Coal Co. Ltd. Astley Green Colliery, Astley Green.
Seymour Clarke	0-6-0ST OC Reb	FW AE	279	1885 1902	13 × 20	3' 5"	Fox Walker class 'B1'. On Tyneside 1885, to Llanelly 1886; to GWR 969.
No. 104 Inveravon	0-4-0ST OC	AB	199	1879	14 × 22	3' 7"	New to Scott & Best, Leith; on L&MM c.9/1887. Boiler exploded 28/3/1889.
Jeannie Waddell	0-6-0ST IC Reb	P AE	464	1888 1898	16 × 22	4' 0"	Peckett class 'X' New to Llanelly 21/9/1888; to Great Mountain Colliery, 7/1913.
—	0-6-0ST IC	P	475	1889	believed 16 × 22	4' 0"	to Llanelly 1889, sold 7/1896. See note in text.
Burntisland	0-4-0ST OC Reb	BH AE	884	1889 1899/ 1904	12 × 19	3' 3"	1890 to Happerfield & Willans, Newport, Mon., by 1913.
Great Mountain	0-6-0T IC	AE	1448	1902	17 × 24	4' 0"	New 4/1902 to GWR 944
George Waddell	0-6-0T IC	AB	1111	1907	17½ × 24	4' 6"	New 8/1907 to GWR 312
E.J. Robertson Grant	0-6-0ST OC	AB	1157	1908	14 × 22	3' 8"	New 8/1908. Left L&MM in 1919. Scrapped prior to 1923.

Name	Type		Builder	Maker's No.	Built	Cyls	Driving Wheels	Remarks
Ravelston	0–6–0T	IC	HC	930	1911	16 × 24	4' 0"	New to GWR 803; BR class '2F'.
John Waddell	0–6–0ST	OC	HC	912	1911	15 × 22	3' 7"	New 17/7/1912 to Great Mountain Colliery, Tumble, c1919.
Merkland	0–6–0T	IC	HC	977	1912	17½ × 26	4' 6"	New 30/4/1912 to GWR 937; number not carried & loco Wdn 6/1923.
Tarndune	0–6–0T	IC	HC	1032	1913	18 × 26	4' 6"	New 18/7/1913 to GWR 339.
Hilda	0–6–0ST	OC	HC	1214	1917	15 × 22	3' 7"	New 26/6/1917 to GWR 359; BR class '1F'.
Victory	0–6–0T	IC	MW	1982	1920	16 × 24		New 3/1920 to GWR 704. Acquired by L&MMR but funded by J. Waddell & Sons at 7% interest.

John Waddell was also proprietor of the Great Mountain Colliery at Tumble, so there may have been some interchange of locos from L&MM to colliery duties at times. An 0–6–0T built by Hudswell Clarke and named Minnie is reputed to have worked on the L&MM c.World War I, but no evidence has been found for or against this suggestion.

Note: Builders' abbreviations
AB   Andrew Barclay
AE   Avonside
BH   Black, Hawthorn
FW   Fox, Walker
HC   Hudswell, Clarke
MW   Manning, Wardle

Table Two

SUMMARY OF LOCOMOTIVES OF THE
LLANELLY AND MYNYDD MAWR RAILWAY TAKEN OVER BY THE GWR

LMM	Wheel	GWR	Builder	Maker's No.	Built	GW Diag.	With-drawn
George Waddell	0–6–0T	312	Andrew Barclay	1111	1907	B45	12/34†
Tarndune	"	339	Hudswell, Clarke	1032	1913	B37	8/43
Hilda	"	359	Hudswell, Clarke	1214	1917	B34	3/54
Victory	"	704	Manning, Wardle	1982	1910	—	1/44
Ravelston	"	803	Hudswell, Clarke	930	1911	B38	31/3/51
Merkland	"	937	Hudswell, Clarke	977	1912	—	6/23
Great Mountain	"	944	Avonside	1448	1902	—	11/28*
Seymour Clarke	"	969	Fox, Walker	279	1875	—	8/25

†312 sold to Robt. Fraser & Sons, 19/1/35. Resold Broomhill Collieries Ltd, 8/35.
*944 sold to Carlton Colliery Association, 9/11/28, and transferred to Hatfield Main colliery, 6/2/29.

TABLE OF CLASS DIMENSIONS

Diagram	Eng. No.	Cylinders	Cyls	Frames	Driving wheels	Heating surface	Grate area	Tank capacity	Boiler pressure	Tractive effort
B.34	359	15 × 22	O	I	3′ 7½″	615.32	10.7	600	160	15475
B.37	339	17½ × 26	I	I	4′ 6″	1194.0	17.5	1180	160	20055
B.38	803	16 × 24	I	I	4′ 0″	1023.5	16.76	1100	160	17410
B.45	312	17½ × 24	I	I	4′ 6″	1157.0	17.2	1150	160	18510
	704	16 × 24	I	I	4′ 0″			900	160	17410
	937	17½ × 26	I	I	4′ 6″			1000	160	20055
B.50	944	17 × 24	I	I	4′ 0″		15.8	900	160	19650
	969									
*B.59	803	16 × 24	I	I	4′ 0″	1023.5	16.76	1100	160	17410

Diagram	Weight Full T.C.	Empty T.C.	Tank
B.34	34.9	27.1	Saddle
B.37	45.18	36.17	Side
B.38	41.3	33.14	"
B.45	45.11	36.17	"
	40.0	32.0	"
	45.10	35.10	"
B.50	42.5	34.0	Side
*B.59	40.12	33.14	"

*Fitted at Swindon with vacuum brake with auxiliary ejector and steam heating apparatus fitted 23/1/31, to work Cleobury Mortimer and Ditton Priors Railway.

Table Three

SUMMARY OF L&MMR CARRIAGE STOCK, 1922 (AFTER E.R. MOUNTFORD)

No.	Whs.	Type	Compartments 1	2	3	G	L	Body	Maker or S/h	Date	GW No.	Renumd.	Withdrawn
1	4	Third			5			27–0	Metro Ry S/h	1913	—	—	9/9/1923
2	4	"			5			"	" " "	"	—	—	12/8/1923
3	4	"			5			"	" " "	"	—	—	12/8/1923
4	4	"			5			"	" " "	"	—	—	9/9/1923
5	4	Bk Third			3	1	Co	"	" " "	"	—	—	12/8/1923
6	4	Third			5			"	" " "	"	—	—	12/8/1923
7	4	Bk Third			3	1	Co	"	" " "	"	—	—	12/8/1923
8	4	Third			5			"	" " "	"	—	—	9/9/1923
9	4	Bk Third			3	1	Co	"	" " "	"	—	—	9/9/1923

NOTE – One source quotes No. 9 as being numbered 9A. This is thought to have been obtained via the Bute Works Supply Co., Cardiff, in the autumn of 1913.

Table Four

L&MMR CONDEMNED WAGON STOCK MOVED TO SWINDON

LMM	GW	Type	Condemned	
1	—	8T Open	14/6/24	
4	—	8T Open	11/8/23	
5	—	8T Open	11/8/23	
10	—	8T Open	11/8/23	
13	—	10T Open	11/8/23	
16	—	8T Open	11/8/23	
21	—	8T Open	11/8/23	
22	—	8T Open	11/8/23	
24	—	8T Open	11/8/23	
36	—	8T Open	11/8/23	
62	—	8T Open	11/8/23	
112	—	8T Open	11/8/23	} Register records two nos. 112.
112	—	8T Open	14/6/24	
113	—	10T Open	11/8/23	
114	—	10T Open	4/10/24	
115	—	10T Open	1/11/24	
117	—	10T Open	11/8/23	
118	—	10T Open	4/10/24	
?	—	8T Open	11/8/23	} LMM nos. not recorded.
?	—	10T Open	11/8/23	
?	—	8T Open	11/8/23	
1	—	Pilot	11/8/23	(Goods Brake Van)
5	—	GBV	6/10/23	
6	—	GBV	3/11/23	
20	—	GBV	9/9/23	
2	—	10T Van	9/9/23	
3	—	10T Van	9/9/23	
4	—	10T Van	9/9/23	
12	—	Tool Van	3/11/23	
15	—	8T Van	11/8/23	
16	—	8T Van	20/5/23	
18	—	8T Van	20/5/23	Also recorded as condemned 11/8/23.
19	—	10T Van	9/9/23	
30	—	8T Van	11/8/23	
116	—	10T Van	14/6/24	
?	—	8T Van	11/8/23	} LMM nos. not recorded.
?	—	8T Van	11/8/23	

PRO Kew 254/357. Courtesy Welsh Railways Research Circle

because on 28th March, 1889, it was damaged beyond repair when the boiler exploded.

For a time the Andrew Barclay number 221 appears to have worked alone, until it was joined in 1886 by *Seymour Clarke*. This 0–6–0 saddle tank was built by Fox, Walker & Co. of Bristol (works number 279 of 1875) and returned to that city in 1903 for rebuilding by the Avonside Engine Co., at which time it was repainted in 'Indian red'. In 1923 *Seymour Clarke* was one of five L & MM engines sent to Swindon for repairs by the GWR, but although it was due to be renumbered as No. 969 it was instead scrapped in July 1925.

A standard Peckett 0–6–0 saddle tank (works number 464 of 1888) was the next arrival on the L & MMR, and by the time it had been put into service in 1889 it had been given the name *Jeannie Waddell*. After rebuilding by Avonside in 1898, it was transferred to the Great Mountain colliery for shunting in July 1913. In 1917 it was sold for further service at the Byfield ironstone quarries in Northamptonshire, but it was broken up in 1923. A similar Peckett (works number 475) was dispatched to John Waddell & Sons at Llanelly in 1889, although a confusing entry in Peckett records has raised doubts as to whether this engine ever reached the L & MMR. The issue is unresolved.

A Black, Hawthorn 0–4–0 saddle tank (works number 884 of 1889) was added to L & MM stock in 1890. Named *Burntisland* this engine is thought to have been employed on a Waddell contract in Fife before transfer to Llanelly. After rebuilding by Avonside in both 1899 and 1904, this locomotive was sold to Messrs Happerfield & Willans of Newport in or about 1913. It was eventually sold for scrap in July, 1931, to J. Cashmore Ltd, Newport.

After 1902 all the locomotives acquired for the L & MMR were six-coupled tank engines, and only two were disposed of prior to the grouping of 1923. The Avonside Engine Co. was clearly in favour at the turn of the century, and they provided *Great Mountain* (works number 1448). Delivered in April 1902, this engine received some modest alterations at the hands of the Great Western, including enlargement of the bunker and the fitting of GWR safety valves. More surprisingly, it retained a reddish brown livery with its painted name until withdrawn by the GWR in 1928. Early in the following year it was sold for further service at Hatfield Main Colliery in Yorkshire, where it became *Hatfield No. 4*. It was scrapped in 1968, when it was the last of the L & MM locomotives.

Two more Andrew Barclay locomotives reached the L & MM in 1907/8. *George Waddell* (works number 1111) arrived in August 1907, and was deemed worthy of reconstruction at Swindon when sent there after the grouping. It emerged in 1927 with a Great Western smokebox, safety valves and boiler, as well as an extended bunker. Numbered 312, it served in the Llanelly area until sold in January 1935. In August of that year it passed to Broomhill Collieries Ltd, of Northumberland, and it was broken up there in April 1961, still carrying the number 312. It managed to carry the name *George Waddell* in its days with the NCB. The other Barclay, *E.J. Robertson Grant*, (works number 1157) went to Llanelly when new in 1908 and seems to have left in 1919. Perhaps the only remarkable feature of this engine was provided by the name; E.J. Robertson Grant was a brother-in-law in the Waddell family, and was reputed to have held the record for motoring from

The Avonside 0–6–0T *Great Mountain* (No. 1448) seen here as built and painted in works grey.   *Locomotive Magazine*

Locomotive *Great Mountain* seen here in Yorkshire as *Hatfield No. 4* in 1949.   *F. Jones*

0-6-0 *Tarndune* in original condition. Oakwood Collection

GWR No. 339 (formerly *Tarndune* of the L&MMR) seen here with Swindon fittings. *J. Lowe*

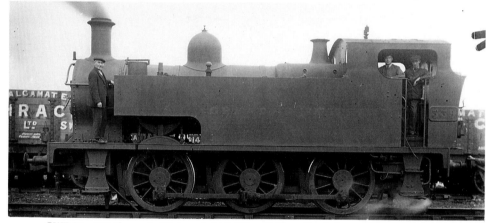

GWR No. 704 (formerly *Victory*, L&MMR) at Dyffryn Yard, Port Talbot, in 1941. *J. Lowe*

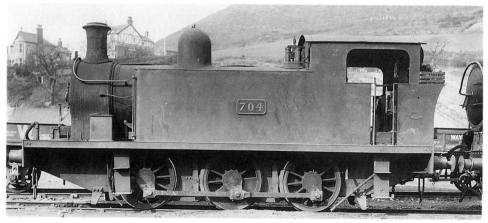

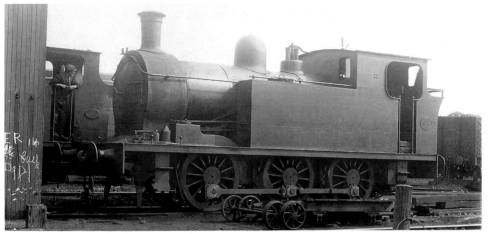

Llanelly & Mynydd Mawr Railway 0–6–0T, *George Waddell*.   *Oakwood Collection*

George Waddell photographed in April, 1958, at NCB Broomhill colliery, Northumberland, note the unusual lettering on the tank side i.e. (ex GWR 312).

F. Jones

0–6–0 L & MMR *Ravelston* in original condition; note the large overhang at the front of the frames.   *Oakwood Collection*

Two pictures of 0–6–0 GWR No. 803, formerly *Ravelston* on the Llanelly & Mynydd
Mawr Railway, at Danygraig shed, Swansea in July 1947.   H.C. Casserley

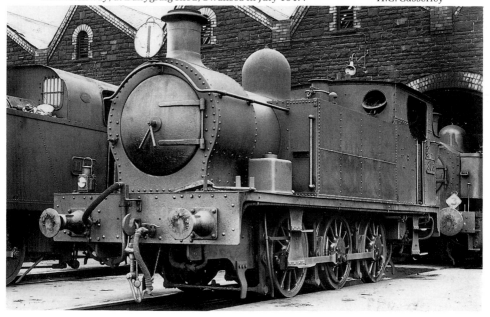

Hudswell Clarke 0–6–0ST *Hilda* seen here as GWR 359 at Danygraig shed on 7th July, 1947.   *H.C. Casserley*

The other side of *Hilda*, minus dome cover, but plus shunting bell; seen here at Danygraig in August, 1950.   *Author's Collection*

Lands End to John o'Groats before World War I.

The locomotive names *Ravelston*, *Merkland* and *Tarndune* were all de-
rived from the names of Waddell family homes. *Ravelston* was a side-tank
built in Leeds by Hudswell, Clarke (works number 930 of 1911). Like other
subsequent L & MM engines, it carried nameplates, and was painted a shade
described in the Hudswell, Clarke order books as 'Midland red'. The livery
has also been described as a deep reddish brown. *Ravelston* was sent to
Swindon very soon after *George Waddell* in 1923, and emerged four years
later having received typical Swindon treatment. In its 'Great Westernised'
state *Ravelston* carried the number 803, and in 1931 was based at Kidder-
minster and regularly worked over the Cleobury Mortimer & Ditton Priors
Light Railway. By 1934 it had moved to Danygraig, and it spent the remainder of its career shunting in sidings near Swansea Docks. As this involved
activity near public roads, it was fitted with a warning bell. *Ravelston*
survived into the British Railways era, but was withdrawn in 1951.

Hudswell, Clarke also provided the second locomotive to be named *John
Waddell* (works number 912 of 1912). After only about seven years this
saddle tank was transferred to the Great Mountain Colliery where it remained until 1959. It was then moved to Morlais colliery, Llangennoch, but
is thought to have done relatively little work there before being scrapped in
September 1964. At least one nameplate from *John Waddell* is known to
have survived.

By now Hudswell, Clarke had become established as the preferred source
of the L & MM's engines. *Merkland* (works number 977 of 1912) had side
tanks extending to the front of the smokebox, with a section cut away for
ease of maintenance. Rather surprisingly, for a relatively young engine, the
Great Western decided it was only fit for scrap. Accordingly it was cut up in
June 1923, without ever having carried its allotted number, 937. An almost
identical engine, *Tarndune*, fared much better. Built by Hudswell, Clarke in
1913 (works number 1032), it went to Swindon in 1923 to await its turn for
modifications very similar to those carried out on *George Waddell* and
Ravelston. As GWR No. 339 it returned to Llanelly at the end of 1926, and
lasted until August 1943, when it was sent for scrap at Caerphilly.

Hilda was virtually the twin of the second *John Waddell*, but became
much better known. In its L & MM days this Hudswell, Clarke product
(works number 1214 of 1917) is said to have been the usual charge of a well
known lay preacher; in short *Hilda* was in safe hands! However in 1924 it
was dispatched to Swansea Docks for shunting duties, and like *Ravelston*,
acquired a bell. As GWR No. 359 it remained at Swansea for many years, and
was not withdrawn by British Railways until February 1954 – the last
L & MM engine in main line stock. As with *John Waddell*, at least one
nameplate has survived.

As has been seen, in 1920 an agreement was made whereby the L & MMR
made financial provision for the acquisition of the contractor's plant and
stock. The arrangement was only finally fulfilled by the GWR in 1923, but
one locomotive was acquired new for the L & MMR. This was *Victory*, built
by Manning, Wardle & Co. in 1920 (works number 1982). The nameplates
were soon discarded by the GWR, and it became number 704. It travelled

widely in South Wales, but was withdrawn in December 1943 and cut up at Caerphilly soon after.

The locomotives of Nevill Druce & Co worked the Stradey Estate line, adjoining the L&MMR. This Peckett saddle tank is shown steaming along Nevill, Druce & Co's own line in the streets south of the Great Western main line. Such workings were once a common sight in this part of Llanelly.   *Llanelli Public Library*

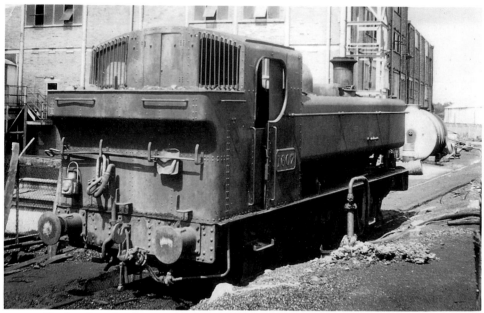

The last Swindon built steam locomotive in commercial service west of Swansea: 0–6–0PT No. 1607 at Cynheidre colliery on 29th July, 1966.   *Michael Hale*

Four-wheel Sentinel locomotive No. 9572 of 1954 seen here at Great Mountain colliery on 15th April, 1960.   *J.A. Peden*

Hawthorn Leslie 0−4−0ST, *Tony* captured on film at Blaenhirwaun colliery in 1962.
F. *Jones*

Avonside No. 1575 of 1910 was employed at both Blaenhirwaun and Great Mountain collieries. It was photographed at NCB Felin Fran on 19th April, 1957.　　*K.P. Plant*

STATISTICS.

ACCOUNTS.

YEAR ENDING DECEMBER 31, 1921.

Capital issued (including nominal additions)—

	£
Loans and debenture stock ..	45,000
Ordinary stock	59,300
	£104,300

Capital expenditure—

Year ending December 31, 1921 ..	16,746
Total to ditto	128,312
	£145,058

Revenue receipts and expenditure of the whole undertaking—

Receipts, including those under the terms of the agreement with the Government in respect of the control of railways (January 1 to August 15, 1921) 55,012
Expenditure 43,530

Net receipts £11,482
Proportion of the amount receivable under Section 11, Railway Act, 1921 4,250
Miscellaneous receipts (net) 1,110

£5,360

Total net income £16,842
Dividend—Nil.

GROSS RECEIPTS.

Year.	Amount.	Year.	Amount.
	£		£
1883	836	1913	17,669
1888	2,392	1917	16,181
1894	4,622	1919	30,126
1903	7,285	1920	47,412
1908	10,985	1921	55,012

MILEAGE.

First track.	Sidings reduced to single track.	Total.
M. Ch.	M. Ch.	M. Ch
13 5	3 25	16 30

NUMBER OF PASSENGERS ORIGINATING ON THE COMPANY'S SYSTEM.

	1921.	1920.
Workmen	129,521	136,566

TONNAGE OF FREIGHT TRAFFIC CARRIED OVER THE COMPANY'S LINES.

Year.	Goods.	Other Minerals.	Coal.	Total.
1883	1,361	18,257	- -	19,618
1888	2,656	48,661	- --	51,317
1894	6,007	70,540	—	76,547
1903	7,884	134,586	—	142,470
1908	13,246	197,106	—	210,352
1913	19,535	8,488	343,079	371,102
1917	17,272	32,987	288,882	339,141
1919	27,544	23,117	314,850	365,511
1920	23,717	29,845	363,815	417,377
1921*	12,745	22,873	299,632	335,250

* Three months' national coal strike.

TONNAGE OF THE PRINCIPAL CLASSES OF MINERAL AND MERCHANDISE CARRIED BY GOODS TRAIN, ORIGINATING ON THE COMPANY'S SYSTEM.

	1921. Tons.	1920. Tons.
Ashes	29	786
Bricks	3,792	3,865
Cement	4	2
Cast-iron pipes	6	6
Flour	17	131
Iron bars	13	4
Locomotive parts ..	51	—
Pitwood	504	771
Rails	86	98
Sand	52	103
Scrap	13	174
Sleepers	3	4
Stone	360	—
Timber	51	—
Total	4,981	5,944

ROLLING-STOCK.

Tank engines	8
Passenger carriages (for workmen)	8
Open wagons (8-12 tons)	24
Covered wagons (8-12 tons)	12
Brake vans	3

LAND PROPERTY (not forming part of the Railway or Stations.)

Labouring class dwellings	7

Chapter Eleven
Under the Great Western

In 1922 and 1923 there was heavy traffic on the Mynydd Mawr line, and Llanelly North Dock was kept busy with coal shipments. Unfortunately this boom did not endure, and a remarkable series of colliery company mergers started in the anthracite coalfield of South Wales. By the end of 1923 the newly formed Amalgamated Anthracite Collieries Co. Ltd owned 10 collieries, and had issued £1,789,000 in shares out of an authorised capital of £2½ million. Meanwhile the Great Mountain Colliery Co., which had a controlling interest in the New Dynant Colliery Co., also acquired the two mines belonging to the Ammanford Colliery Co. In June 1924, this enlarged undertaking was purchased by the United Anthracite Collieries Co., giving this combine a total output of about 600,000 tons per annum, and an authorised capital of £2½ million. At this date South Wales anthracite production amounted to about 5 million tons, of which the two major mergers – A.A.C. and United Anthracite – controlled about one quarter. In 1925, following further colliery acquisition, United Anthracite alone had almost one fifth of Welsh anthracite output.

Britain returned to the Gold Standard in 1925, and a depressed coal export trade sagged further, causing deeper financial worries for the industry. The 1926 General Strike, and associated industrial unrest, made matters worse. The dispute in the South Wales coalfield halted all the collieries served by the L&MM line for several months. The South Wales Miners' Federation had lodges at Great Mountain, Cross Hands, Blaenhirwaun and Mynydd Sylen, but by this date the Caeglas colliery appears to have been out of use. Suffice to say that traffic on the railway slumped, and indeed stopped altogether in May, at the time of the General Strike.

The mood at Tumble in these painful days has been well described by Glyn Anthony in his book *Coal Dust and Dogma*, (1987). As hardship increased, so did instances of the theft of essential items like fuel. This problem appears to have been most noticeable in Llanelly: one of the Mynydd Mawr stages was stripped of its decking, and coal thefts at the North Dock became more frequent. The one light moment in this unhappy period could have been catastrophic. On 5th May, at the start of the General Strike, special constables were told to open the gates at Old Castle to allow a fish train to pass. Instead of going to the crossing on the Great Western main line, they opened the gates on the L&MM line alongside the Old Castle tinplate works. A few minutes later the main line gates were smashed to pieces by the train!

The severe problems of the anthracite industry continued, and in 1927 United Anthracite was taken over by A.A.C., the authorised share capital of which was increased to £5 million. As a result A.A.C. controlled 23 collieries producing about 40 per cent of Welsh anthracite output. However, the enlarged A.A.C. did not run all the pits in its own name. On 17th November, 1927, the Great Mountain Collieries Co. Ltd. was reconstituted as a wholly owned subsidiary of Amalgamated Anthracite, and although it might appear that this ended Waddell family involvement, it is believed that for many

Up Trains. LLANELLY TO CROSS HANDS. Week Days.

Distance from Old Castle Crossing M.C.	STATION.	1 MX Goods. arr. A.M.	1 Goods. dep. A.M.	2 M Workmen. arr. A.M.	2 Workmen. dep. A.M.	3	4 M Goods. arr. A.M.	4 Goods. dep. A.M.	5 M Goods. arr. A.M.	5 Goods. dep. A.M.	6	7	8 M Goods. arr. P.M.	8 Goods. dep. P.M.	9	10 M Goods. arr. P.M.	10 Goods. dep. P.M.	11
	Old Castle Crossing																	
30	Old Castle Junction		9 15					8 30		8 50				1 30			1 40	
60	Sandy			6 34	6 30													
1 30	Furnace			6 38	6 35													
2 0	Felin Foel				5 43													
4 1	Bynea Colliery																	
5 20	Eclipse Brick Works			5 52	5 53													
8 20	Horeb	9 55		6 0	6 1		9 10	8 20	9 30	9 35			9 0	2 0		2 20	1 40	
8 60	Cynheidre			6 20			9 40	8 90	9 55	10 0			9 30	2 10		2 90	2 20	
11 10	Cwmblawd			6 27	6 24		9 55	9 45	10 5	10 0			9 55	2 40		9 50	3 0	
12 60	Tumble			6 30	6 28											8 10		
	S. & R. Colliery																	
	Cross Hands																	

STATION.	12	13 M	14 M Goods. arr. P.M.	14 Goods. dep. P.M.	15	16 M Goods. arr. P.M.	16 Goods. dep. P.M.	17	18	19	20 M Goods. arr. P.M.	20 Goods. dep. P.M.	21 M Goods. arr. P.M.	21 Goods. dep. P.M.	22	23
Old Castle Crossing																
Old Castle Junction				1 40			7 0							8 30		
Sandy			1 50													
Furnace																
Felin Foel																
Bynea Colliery																
Eclipse Brick Works																
Horeb						7 40								9 20		
Cynheidre													9 10	9 30		
Cwmblawd													9 40	9 50		
Tumble													10 0			

Great Western working timetable for 1927.

Down Trains.   CROSS HANDS TO LLANELLY.   **Week Days.**

Distance from Cross Hands M.C.	STATION.	1 M Goods. arr. A.M.	dep. A.M.	2 G Engine and Van. M X arr.	dep.	3 M Goods. arr. A.M.	dep. A.M.	4 M Goods. arr. A.M.	dep. A.M.	5 arr.	dep.	6 M Goods. arr. A.M.	dep. A.M.	7 M Goods. arr. P.M.	dep. P.M.	8 M Workmen's. 80 arr. P.M.	dep. P.M.	9 M Goods. arr. P.M.	dep. P.M.	10 arr.	dep.	11 arr.	dep.
—	Cross Hands	—	—	—	—	—	—	—	—	…	…	—	10 40	—	—	—	—	—	—	…	…	…	…
1 40	G. & R. Colliery	9 50	9 40	…	8 0	10 44	10 20	11 37	11 10	…	…	—	—	—	—	2 60	2 40	…	4 15	…	…	…	…
3 70	Tumble	10 30	10 20	…	—	—	10 57	11 27	11 50	…	…	11 10	11 93	—	—	2 70	2 66	4 39	4 52	…	…	…	…
6 30	Cwmblawd	P10 35	P10 33	…	—	11 12	P11 17	12 5	P12 10	…	…	—	—	—	—	5 10	3 12	…	…	…	…	…	…	…
7 30	Cynheidre Stop Board	11 0	P11 0	…	—	—	—	—	—	…	…	—	—	—	—	5 15	3 18	…	…	…	…	…	…	…
8 49	Horeb	—	—	…	—	—	—	—	—	…	…	—	—	—	—	—	—	…	…	…	…	…	…
8 60	Eclipse Brick Works	10 55	—	…	—	11 37	P11 42	12 30	P12 35	…	…	11 88	P11 48	—	—	5 22	3 24	5 33	7 P5 12	…	…	…	…
9 10	Bylen Colliery	—	—	…	—	11 45	—	12 38	—	…	…	—	—	—	1 40	3 88	3 28	—	—	…	…	…	…
10 60	Stop Board	—	—	…	—	—	—	—	—	…	…	12 8	P12 8	—	—	—	—	5 33	P5 37	…	…	…	…
11 20	Felin Foel	—	—	…	—	—	—	—	—	…	…	—	—	—	—	—	—	—	—	…	…	…	…
11 48	Furnace	—	—	…	—	—	—	—	—	…	…	12 11	—	1 50	—	3 30	—	5 40	—	…	…	…	…
12 0	Sandy	11 5	P11 0	…	3·30?	—	—	—	—	…	…	—	—	—	—	—	—	—	—	…	…	…	…

STATIONS.	12 M Workmen's. SX arr. P.M.	dep. P.M.	13 M Goods. arr. P.M.	dep. P.M.	14 arr.	dep.	15 arr.	dep.	16 M Goods. arr. P.M.	dep. P.M.	17 arr.	dep.	18 G Engine and Van. arr. P.M.	dep. P.M.	19 arr.	dep.	20 G Engine and Van. arr. P.M.	dep. P.M.	21 arr.	dep.	22 M Goods. arr. P.M.	dep. P.M.	23 arr.
Cross Hands	—	8 40	—	4 35	…	…	…	…	—	4 55	…	…	—	—	…	…	—	—	…	…	—	10 30	—
G. & R. Colliery	3 50	3 55	—	—	…	…	…	…	5 28	5 38	…	…	—	7·45	…	…	—	9·15	…	…	10 33	11 0	…
Tumble	4 10	4 12	5 2	5 15	…	…	…	…	—	—	…	…	—	—	…	…	—	—	…	…	11 8	12 0	…
Cwmblawd	4 15	4 18	—	—	…	…	…	…	—	—	…	…	—	—	…	…	—	—	…	…	12 24	12 37	…
Cynheidre Stop Board	—	—	—	—	…	…	…	…	—	—	…	…	—	—	…	…	—	—	…	…	—	—	…
Horeb	—	—	—	—	…	…	…	…	—	—	…	…	—	—	…	…	—	—	…	…	—	—	…
Eclipse Brick Works	4 22	4 24	5 30	P5 35	…	…	…	…	5 53	P5 58	…	…	—	—	…	…	—	—	…	…	12 53	P1 257	…
Bylen Colliery	4 28	—	—	—	…	…	…	…	—	—	…	…	—	—	…	…	—	—	…	…	—	—	…
Stop Board	—	—	5 55	P6 0	…	…	…	…	6 18	P6 23	…	…	—	—	…	…	—	—	…	…	1 17	P1 22	…
Felin Foel	—	4 30	—	—	…	…	…	…	—	—	…	…	—	—	…	…	—	—	…	…	—	—	…
Furnace	—	—	—	—	…	…	…	…	—	—	…	…	—	—	…	…	—	—	…	…	—	—	…
Stop Board	—	—	6 8	6 8	…	…	…	…	6 30	—	…	…	—	—	…	…	—	—	…	…	1 25	—	…
Sandy	—	—	—	—	…	…	…	…	—	—	…	…	—	—	…	…	—	—	…	…	—	—	…

years the younger John Waddell was on the board of A.A.C. In 1928 A.A.C. expanded even further with the acquisition of three other coal companies – Hendersons Welsh Anthracite, and the Llewellyn group.

Between 1924 and 1928 the average export price for anthracite fell by 27 per cent, but by 1930 both the European and the Canadian markets were growing. Accordingly output began to increase, although for several years even the powerful but over-capitalised A.A.C. was not able to pay a dividend. At Blaenhirwaun, near Cross Hands, S. & R. Anthracite Collieries Ltd. was obliged to go into liquidation, notwithstanding their good reputation as employers. In April 1932, the colliery was taken over by an A.A.C. subsidiary, the New Blaenhirwaun Colliery Co.

This dominance of the local coal industry by Amalgamated Anthracite was not without benefits for the railway. Previously each coal company had preferred to use its own private owner wagons. This gave rise to numerous difficulties as the railway company tried to provide each pit with the required number of the appropriate wagons at the time requested. At busy periods, in an improving market, the congestion could cause chaos, even to the extent of compelling collieries to halt production until wagons were available. The local explanation for these idle days at the pits was 'stop-trucks'. Such difficulties were reduced by the emergence of A.A.C., because as most of the wagons came into one ownership the business of marshalling and distributing wagons was greatly simplified.

The earliest Great Western working timetable to come to light shows train services operating in the summer of 1927. The timetable is especially noteworthy in showing the workmen's service. This was scheduled to leave Sandy at 5.30 am, with the return service arriving back at Sandy at 5.40 pm on weekdays, or 3.15 pm on Saturdays. By this time several L&MMR locomotives had been sent to Swindon for disposal or reconstruction, and Great Western '1901' class 0–6–0 tank engines had been introduced on some trains. Only three L&MM locomotives appear to have returned to the line after visiting Swindon, namely *George Waddell*, *Tarndune* and *Victory*, although *Ravelston* may have put in a brief appearance. On some heavy trains of pit timber one locomotive would be on the front, and up to three more might be on the back, banking. Although these engines on occasions might form two trains for the return journey, separated on a time interval basis, it was also quite common for the coal to come down with three locomotives on the front, and one at the back. The Great Western pannier tanks employed included Nos. 1941, 2002 and 2027. About once a year a larger locomotive – thought to have been a Dean Goods – went up the Mynydd Mawr line with a Great Western inspection saloon. At Tumble and Cross Hands this ensemble was regarded as the railway event of the year, and always attracted the interest of local schoolchildren.

During the 1930s the export of anthracite increased, and the Canadian market became especially important to the Great Mountain colliery. In the winter months, when shipments were suspended by the freezing of the St Lawrence River, it became customary to stockpile tens of thousands of tons of coal in the storage area between the colliery and the Mynydd Mawr line. When the thaw came in the spring, and the river was reopened, vessels

Up Trains.

LLANELLY TO CROSS HANDS.
SINGLE LINE.
Week Days.

Mileage M.C. Mile Post	STATION	Time Allowances for Freight Trains — Point to Point Times Mins.	Allow for Stop Mins.	Allow for Start Mins.	Goods A.M. arr.	Goods A.M. dep.	Goods A.M. arr.	Goods A.M. dep.	Goods P.M. arr.	Goods P.M. dep.	Goods K P.M. arr.	Goods K P.M. dep.	Goods K P.M. arr.	Goods K P.M. dep.
0 10	Old Castle Crossing	—			…	…	…	…	…	…	…	…	…	…
0 35	Old Castle Junction	—	—	—	…	7 45	…	…	…	12 0	…	12 20	…	…
0 68	Sandy	6	—	1	…	—	…	…	…	—	…	…	…	…
1 53	Furnace	6	—	1	—	—	…	…	…	—	…	…	…	…
2 42	Felin Foel	12	—	1	—	—	…	…	…	—	…	…	…	…
4 77	Sylen Colliery				—	—	…	8 50	…	—	…	…	…	…
5 6	Eclipse Brick Works	8	—	1	—	—	…	—	…	—	…	…	…	…
5 30	Horeb	8	—	—	8 26	8 30	…	—	…	—	…	…	…	…
6 61	Cynheidre	5	2	1	8 47	—	9	9 15	12 41	12 50	1 1	…	…	…
9 9	Cwmblawd	9	—	—	—	9 30	9 7	9	—	—	…	…	…	…
11 27	Tumble	10	—	1	—	—	9 27	10 5	—	—	…	…	…	…
12 39	S. & R. Colliery	5	—	—	—	—	—	—	—	—	…	…	…	…
12 62	Cross Hands M. Sidg.	5			…	…	1 20	1 55	1 20	1 55	…	…	…	…

For distance from Old Castle Crossing, deduct 40 chains.

Down Trains (SW)

Distance from Cross Hands. MS

Distance M.C.	STATION	Time Allowances for Freight Trains — Point to Point times Mins.	Allow for Stop Mins.	Allow for Start Mins.	Goods A.M. arr.	Goods A.M. dep.	Goods A.M. arr.	Goods A.M. dep.	Goods P.M. arr.	Goods P.M. dep.	Goods P.M. arr.	Goods P.M. dep.	Goods P.M. arr.	Goods P.M. dep.
0 33	Cross Hands M. Sidg.	3	1	1	…	…	9 27	10 5	1 20	1 55	…	2 15	…	2 35
3 35	S. & R. Colliery	8	1	1	8 47	9 30	—	—	—	—	…	…	—	—
3 53	Tumble	6	1	1	—	10 7	10 31	10 48	2 21	2 38	2 41	2 58	3 1	3 18
6 1	Cwmblawd	8	1	2	9 15	—	—	—	—	—	—	—	—	—
—	Cynheidre Stop Board	5	1	1	—	—	—	—	—	—	—	—	—	—
7 32	Horeb	—	1	1	10 25	P10 30	11 6	P11 11	2 56	P3 1	3 16	P3 21	3 36	P3 41
7 57	Eclipse Brick Works	6	1	2	—	—	—	—	—	—	—	—	—	—
7 65	Sylen Colliery	4	1	1	—	—	—	—	—	—	—	—	—	—
—	Stop Board	8	1	—	—	—	—	—	—	—	—	—	—	—
10 20	Felin Foel	8	1	—	—	—	11 36	P11 41	3 26	P3 31	3 46	P3 51	4 6	P4 11
11 9	Furnace	6	1	—	10 55	P11 0	11 46	—	8 36	—	3 56	—	4 16	—
—	Stop Board	3	1	1	11 5	—	—	—	—	—	—	—	—	—
11 74	Sandy													

Part of the Great Western working timetable for July 1938.

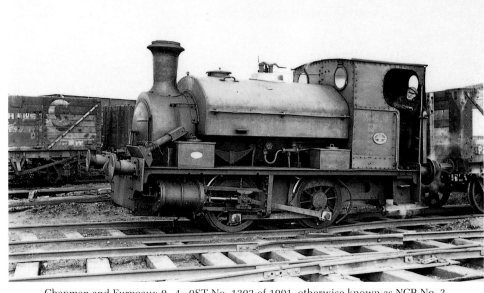

Chapman and Furneaux 0−4−0ST No. 1202 of 1901, otherwise known as NCB No. 2, shunts at New Cross Hands colliery in 1950. *F. Jones*

Edith, a Hudswell, Clarke 0−4−0ST (No. 894 of 1909) at New Cross Hands colliery. *F. Jones*

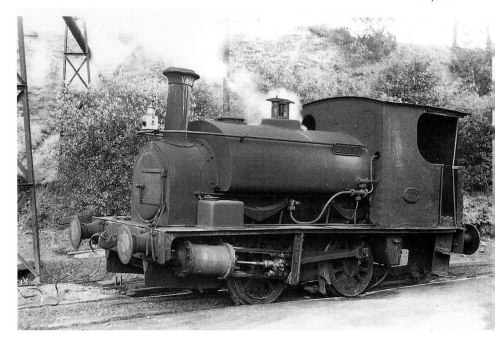

MOUNTAIN BRANCH.

Single Line worked between Tirydail and Foot of Cross Hands Incline by Ordinary Train Staff. Only one Engine at a time (except as shewn on page 323 of Appendix to this Book) is allowed between Down Branch Starting Signal at Tirydail and the Foot of Cross Hands Incline.

UP TRAINS—WEEK DAYS.

M.	C.	STATIONS.		6.40 a.m. Llandilo Jc. Empties.	Empties.	Empties.	Empties.	Empties.
				A.M.	A.M.	A.M.	A.M.	P.M.
—	—	Tirydail	arr.	6 58	8 10	9 25	11 15	1 35
			dep.	7 20	8 35	9 55	12 15	2 30
	63	Plasbach Level Crossing	,,	CR	—	—	P.M.	CR
1	11	Gulston Jct.	,,	CR	—	—	—	CR
1	22	Nantywrach Level Crossing	,,	CR	—	—	—	
1	62	Pantyblodau Level Crossing	,,	—	—	—	—	
2	21	Caerbryn	,,	—	—	—	—	
2	26	Foot of Incline	arr.	7 35	8 50	10 10	12 30	2 45

DOWN TRAINS—WEEK DAYS.

M.	C.	STATIONS.		Coal.	Coal.	Coal.	Coal.	Coal.
				A.M.	A.M.	A.M.	P.M.	P.M.
—	—	Foot of Incline	dep.	7 55	9 10	10 40	1 0	3 15
	5	Caerbryn	,,	—	—	—	—	—
	44	Pantyblodau Level Crossing	,,	—	—	—	—	—
1	0	Stop Board	,,	P	P	P	P	P
1	5	Nantywrach Level Crossing	,,	CR	CR			
1	15	Gulston Jct.	,,	CR	CR	11 10	1 30	3 45
1	43	Plasbach Level Crossing	,,					
2	26	Tirydail	arr.	8 10	9 25	11 15	1 35	3 50
			dep.	8 35	9 55	12 15	2 30	9 45

No carriage or truck load exceeding 9 feet in width, 8 feet 6 inches in height at the Side, or 10 feet 8 inches in height at the Centre above the level of the rail can be taken between the top of the Incline and Cross Hands, as anything exceeding these dimensions will not pass under the bridge.

WORKING ARRANGEMENT ON CROSS HANDS BRANCH WITH THE EMLYN COLLIERY CO.

SINGLE LINE.—Only one Engine at a time allowed on the Cross Hands Branch.

DOWN TRAINS. WEEK DAYS.

		A.M.	A.M.	A.M.	A.M.	A.M.	P.M.	P.M.	P.M.
Mileage Siding	dep.	—	—	8 25	—	—	2 10	—	
Emlyn Junction	,,	7 0	8 0	—	10 30	11 30	1 30		3 0
Top of Incline	arr.	7 5	8 5	8 35	10 35	11 35	1 35	2 20	3 5

UP TRAINS. WEEK DAYS.

		A.M.	A.M.	A.M.	A.M.	P.M.	P.M.	P.M.	P.M.
Top of Incline	dep.	7 25	8 10	8 55	10 55	12 55	1 55	2 40	3 25
Emlyn Junction	arr.	7 30		9 0	11 0	1 0	2 0	2 45	3 30
Mileage Siding	,,		8 20		11 0		2 0		

The Engine must at all times be in front of the Trucks coming from the Colliery or Mileage Siding towards the Incline, and behind the Trucks going from the Top of the Incline to the Colliery or Mileage Siding.

In coming from the Colliery or Mileage Siding, the Train must be brought to a dead stand at the Emlyn Junction with this Line.

Extracts from the GWR July 1938 working timetable.

LLANELLY AND CROSS HANDS. Week Days Only.

SINGLE LINE—Only one Engine at a time allowed.

Up Trains.

M. C.	STATIONS.	Point to Point Times (Mins.)	Allow for Stop (Mins.)	Allow for Start (Mins.)	Ruling gradient 1 in	Freight K (a.m.) arr	Freight K (a.m.) dep	Freight K (a.m.) arr	Freight K (a.m.) dep	Freight K (p.m.) arr	Freight K (p.m.) dep	Freight K (p.m.) arr	Freight K (p.m.) dep	Freight K (p.m.) arr	Freight K (p.m.) dep
0 40	Old Castle Crossing	—	—	—	48 F		7 45		7 45	RR on Saturdays	1 0	RR on Saturdays	1 0		1 20 SX
0 35	Old Castle Junction	—	—	—	55 R										
0 68	Sandy	6	1	1	45 R										
0 53	Furnace	6	1	1	41 R										
2 42	Felin Foel	12	1	1	42 R	Y		Y							
4 77	Sylen Colliery	—	—	—	68 R										
5 30	Eclipse Brick Works	8	1	1	49 R										
6 61	Horeb	8	1	1	41 R	8 27	8 32	8 27	8 52						
6 9	Cynheidre	5	1	1	138 R					Z		Z			
9 —	Cwmblawd	10	1	1	83 R					1 42	1 52	1 42	1 52		
11 27	Tumble	5	1	1	109 R	8 49	8 50	8 49	9 50			2 6	2 8	2 2	2 12
12 39	S. & R. Colliery	5	1	1	191 F			9 24	10 5	2 6	3 25	2 15	2 50	2 29	3 10
12 62	Cross Hands M. Siding												2 8 50		

Down Trains.

M. C. (Distance from Cross Hands M. Siding)	STATIONS.	Point to Point Times (Mins.)	Allow for Stop (Mins.)	Allow for Start (Mins.)	Ruling gradient 1 in	Freight K (a.m.) arr	Freight K (a.m.) dep	Freight K (a.m.) arr	Freight K (a.m.) dep	Freight K (p.m.) arr	Freight K (p.m.) dep	Freight K (p.m.) arr	Freight K (p.m.) dep	Freight K (p.m.) arr	Freight K (p.m.) dep
0 33	Cross Hands M. Siding	3	1	1	191 R	8 49		10 5		SX	3 10				3 50
0 35	S. & R. Colliery	8	1	1	109 R	9 24	9 50	10 20		2 29					
1 33	Tumble	5	1	1	83 F	10 15	P1020 10 35	10 20	P1060	3 25	P340	3 25	P4 10 (RR on Saturdays)	4 0	4 10
3 —	Cwmblawd	8	1	2	119 F	10 35						3 65		P440	
6 77	Cyneheidre Stop Board	5	1	1	41 F						P340		P4 10	4 25 RR (on Saturdays)	
7 7	Horeb	—	—	—	49 F	10 28	P1043	11 8	P1113	3 58	P4 8	3 58	P4 8		
7 65	Eclipse Brick Works	6	1	2	68 F										
—	Sylen Colliery	4	1	1	41 F	10 28	P1043								
—	Stop Board	8	1	2	42 F										
10 20	Felin Foel	8	1	—	45 F	11 8	P1113	11 13	P1113	4 28	P4 33	4 28	P4 33	4 58	P5 3
10 9	Furnace	6	1	—	289 F	11 38	P1113	11 38	P1143	4 38	P5 3	4 58	P5 3	5 28	
11 —	Stop Board	3	1	—											
11 74	Sandy					11 48	P1143	11 48	P1143			5 8		5 38	P5 33

Y—Coupled to Cynheidre. Z—Coupled to S & R. Colliery. Yard Master, Llanelly Dock, to arrange clearance of traffic from Felin Foel Brick Works and Horeb. †—For distance from Old Castle Crossing, deduct 40 chains.

WORKING ARRANGEMENT ON CROSS HANDS BRANCH WITH THE EMLYN COLLIERY CO.

The Engine must at all times be in front of the Trucks coming from the Colliery or Mileage Siding towards the Incline, and behind the Trucks going from the top of the Incline to the Colliery or Mileage Siding.

In coming from the Colliery or Mileage Siding, the Train must be brought to a dead stand at the Emlyn Junction with this Line.

(See Notice N.W. 1536 for full working instructions.)

Part of the GWR working timetable for the Summer, 1949.

WEEKDAYS   LLANELLY AND CROSS HANDS

SINGLE LINE—Worked under "Time interval" System.

DOWN

Mileage from Cross Hands Siding. Gradient column: From previous place mentioned — Ruling Gradient 1 in.

M	C	DOWN	Gradient	K 9475 (am)	K 9475 (am)	K 9475 (PM, SX)	K 9475 (PM, SX)	K 9475 (PM, SX)
—	—	Cross Hands Mineral Sdg. dep	—		10 5			3 50
0	33	S. and R. Colliery .... arr	191 R				2 16	
		... dep					3 25	
1	35	Tumble .... arr	109 R	8 49	10 15	2P29	3 30	4 0
		... dep		9 50	10 20	3 10	3 40	4 10
6	1	Cynheidre Stop Board arr	116 F	10P5	10P35	3P25	3P55	4P25
—	—	... dep / Stop Board .... arr	67 F	10 20	10 50	3 40	4 10	4 40
		... arr		10P38	11P8	3P58	4P28	4P58
—	—	... dep / Stop Board .... arr	45 F	10 43	11 13	4 3	4 33	5 3
		... arr		11P8	11P38	4P28	4P58	5P28
		... dep		11 13	11 43	4 33	5 3	5 33
11	74	Sandy .... arr	41 F	11 18	11 48	4 38	5 8	5 38

UP

Mile Post Mileage. Gradient column: From previous place mentioned — Ruling Gradient 1 in.

M	C	UP	Gradient	K 9491 (am)	K 9414 (am)	K 9414 (PM, SX)	K 9473 (PM, SX)	K 9491 (PM, SX)
0	68	Sandy ... ... dep	—	7 45	7 45	1 0	1 0	1 20
1	53	Furnace	45 R					
2	42	Felin Foel	41 R					
4	77	Sylen Colliery	42 R		N	N	Z	Z
5	5	Eclipse Brick Works	75 R					
5	30	Horeb	49 R					
6	61	Cynheidre ... ... arr	41 R	8 27	8 27	1 42	1 42	2 2
		.... dep		8 32	8 52	1 52	1 52	2 12
11	27	Tumble ... ... arr	83 R	8 49				2 29
		.... dep		9 50				3 10
12	39	S. and R. Colliery ... arr	109 F			2 16	2 16	
		.... dep				2 28	3 25	
12	62	Cross Hands Mineral Sdg. dep / arr	191 F		9 24	2 35		3 25

Right-hand column notes:
Coupled to S. and R. Cly. Yard Master.
Coupled to Cynheidre, Yard Master, for clearance of traffic from Felin Foel Brick Works and Horeb.

British Railways working timetable for the Summer of 1959.

would gather at Swansea and Llanelly to take cargoes of anthracite to Canada. Accordingly the line was often at its busiest in springtime, with extra trains leaving Tumble for the docks almost every day until the storage area was cleared. This valuable traffic was maintained even during World War II, and for a few years afterwards.

In 1930 Llanelly North Dock received a visit from the Danish ship *Bretagne*, which with a cargo capacity of 5,500 tons was the largest to use the dock to that date. However the hazards of navigating the shallow Burry Inlet were such that most vessels using the North Dock were much smaller. At a time when ships were generally increasing in size this did not bode well for the port's future, although the later 1930s might be seen now as the heyday of the Llanelly North Dock. Indeed, in April 1934, the Llanelly Harbour Trust employed no less than 120 people on the North Dock. In the following year the port handled a record 584,696 tons of coal. With such activity at the North Dock at this time, the Harbour Trustees introduced a bye-law banning public bathing in the dock. For those fortunate enough to enjoy less polluted facilities elsewhere this move might seem quite reasonable; in Llanelly in 1935, though, it was described as 'the virtual confiscation of a privilege which has come to be looked upon as a birthright.' In spite of the watchful attention of the police, the controversial bye-law was regularly flouted for many years.

By the mid 1930s there were improvements not only in the coal trade, but also in the iron, steel and tinplate industries. Trade in all these commodities was depressed in the years following the General Strike, and numerous firms experienced protracted periods of short time working. Evidence of the improving outlook came in 1936 with the news that furnaces were to be restarted at the South Wales Steelworks of Richard Thomas & Co. At the time this company was establishing a strip mill at Ebbw Vale, a development which Llanelly tinplate producers viewed with some concern. By November 1938, they had reached an agreement for the amalgamation of five tinplate works in the Llanelly area (one of which was Old Castle) to form the third largest combine in the Welsh tinplate trade. The object of the exercise was to set up their own strip mill, and to keep as much of the trade as possible at Llanelly. In the event the outbreak of war delayed the scheme, and caused it to be reconsidered. Early in 1945 it was reported that four tinplate firms would collaborate to establish a hot strip mill for tinplate and steel at Port Talbot, with additional plant being provided at Llanelly. Two years later it was announced that the Steel Company of Wales would be formed with the cooperation of leading companies to construct the new hot strip mill. By now it was also agreed that cold mills should be erected at Llangyfelach, and Trostre, Llanelly.

During World War II Llanelly docks were used extensively for loading petrol and other fuel, and also for the storage of vast amounts of materials for local works and munitions factories. After the war trade at the North Dock plummeted. Whereas 1,297,037 tons of exports and imports had been handled in the heyday of the North Dock between 1936 and 1939, only 102,000 tons were handled between 1944 and 1947. By the time the GWR was nationalised and became part of British Railways on 1st January, 1948,

A special train conveying railway enthusiasts in open wagons passes Magpie Grove signal box on 25th September, 1965.   *H.C. Casserley*

GWR 0–6–0PT No. 1643 with the same train at Cross Hands.   *H.C. Casserley*

traffic from the Mynydd Mawr line to the North Dock was negligible. It is not known exactly when coal was last taken over the L&MM bridge over the South Wales main line for shipment, but this access to the North Dock was effectively out of use in 1950. By then the North Dock line and some of the L&MM sidings appear to have been used for wagon storage. Trade at the North Dock itself declined further, and the Dock was actually closed by a hard pressed Llanelly Harbour Trust on 10th February, 1951.

At the opposite end of the Mynydd Mawr line other changes were taking place in the area of Cross Hands. For many years the Cross Hands goods depot on the Mountain branch had been situated not at Cross Hands itself, but almost a mile away at Lamb siding, Penygroes, some 3 miles 23 chains from the junction at Tirydail. Indeed, in later years the depot was actually known as 'Cross Hands (for Penygroes)'. The main source of traffic was provided by the important Emlyn colliery nearby, but by 1947 this was closed, effectively terminating the working arrangement whereby GWR traffic above the rope-worked Cross Hands incline was moved by the colliery's engine. It seems unlikely that the incline was ever operated by the nationalised British Railways, and it is believed that for a short time goods for Cross Hands and Penygroes were handled at the siding at the foot of the incline adjoining Caerbryn level crossing. Even this traffic was modest, for in the year ending 31st October, 1949, only 125 tons of general merchandise were sent out, and 89 tons of coal and 20 tons of other goods were received in. As Cross Hands was well served by the L&MM route, it was hardly surprising that the closure of the Mountain branch west of Gulston Junction was proposed in 1950. This section closed officially in November 1950, and the track west of Nantywrach crossing, near Gulston Junction, was lifted in the following year.

In November 1947, the *Railway Observer* published a brief article giving a fascinating glimpse of the L&MM line at the close of the Great Western era. In particular it was noted that the locomotive shed at Sandy had been 'blown down during heavy winds earlier in the year'. In fact it had suffered severe fire damage that winter, and the jobs done there were transferred to the main shed at Llanelly. There were then five booked turns from Sandy each weekday, usually worked by '2021' class tank locomotives. Each morning the pannier tanks came across to Sandy from Llanelly shed with up to three or four coupled together. The engine crews must have had some arrangement with gardeners or allotment holders along the line, because locomotives could sometimes be seen going up the line with great bundles of bean sticks wedged between the safety valve cover and the cab.

On 1st July, 1947, the 7.45 am goods from Sandy comprised 30 empty wagons hauled by No. 2083, and assisted in the rear by No. 2081; this was the maximum load then permitted for two engines working between Sandy and Cynheidre without a stop. After taking water at Cynheidre both engines continued to the S&R colliery, where No. 2081 was left to shunt the wagons, whilst No. 2083 continued to Cross Hands with the brakevan. The maximum load on the easier gradients beyond Cynheidre was then 70 empty wagons. The best evidence of the old L&MM itself was provided by the sight of the engine *John Waddell* shunting the colliery sidings at Tumble. This locomotive had been transferred by the contractors from the L & MMR to the Great Mountain Colliery in 1919, before the railway was taken over by the GWR. It managed to keep the name *John Waddell* alive at Tumble for a full 40 years, before being transferred to Morlais colliery at Llangennech in 1959.

Two locomotives closely associated with the Mynydd Mawr line: No. 1607 (*top*) at Cross Hands on 3rd June, 1953 – *R.C. Riley*; and No. 359 *Hilda* (*bottom*) at Danygraig, Swansea, on 8th September, 1951 – *H.C. Casserley*

A class '37' diesel heads a train of coal empties for Cynheidre over the junction with the L&MM line at Old Castle, 15th June, 1973.   *Author*

Class '37' diesel No. 6869 at Old Castle with a train from Cynheidre to Swansea Docks, 15th June, 1973.   *Author*

A brakevan view of the L&MM line at Furnace on 15th June, 1973. Note the footpath adjacent to the railway. *Author*

With a winding tower at Cynheidre just visible over the trees, a train of coal empties makes for the colliery on 15th June, 1973. *Author*

Diesel No. 6869 shunts at Cynheidre colliery, 15th June, 1973.   *Author*

A railtour at Cynheidre, 9th May, 1987.   *Author*

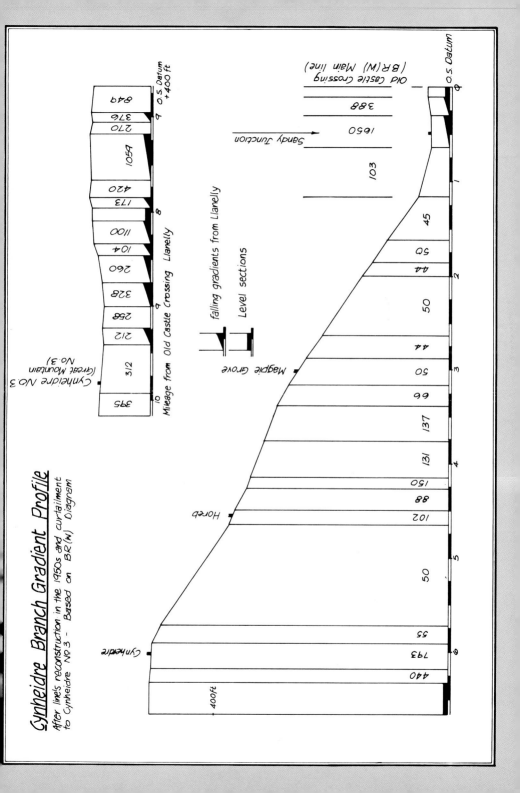

Cynheidre Branch Gradient Profile

After lines reconstruction in the 1950s and curtailment to Cynheidre No 3 - Based on BR(W) Diagram

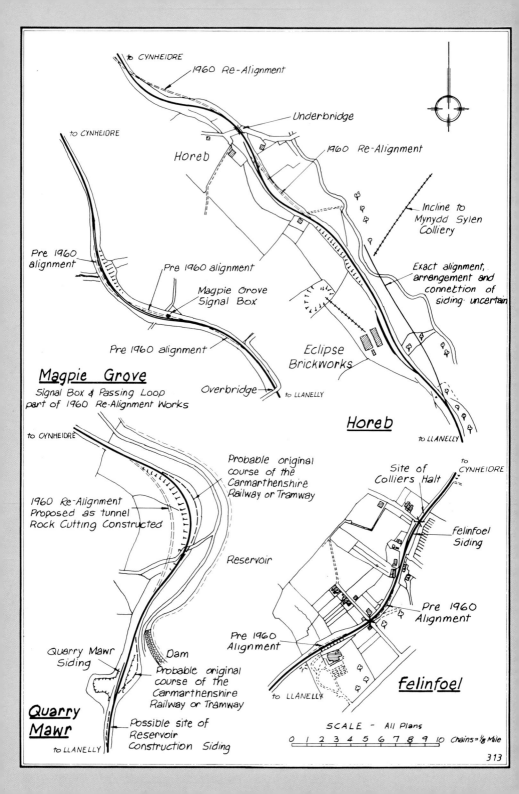

to CYNHEIDRE

1960 Re-Alignment

Underbridge

1960 Re-Alignment

to CYNHEIDRE

Horeb

Incline to
Mynydd Sylen
Colliery

Pre 1960
alignment

Pre 1960 alignment

Magpie Grove
Signal Box

Exact alignment,
arrangement and
connection of
siding uncertain

Pre 1960 alignment

Eclipse
Brickworks

Magpie Grove

Signal Box & Passing Loop
part of 1960 Re-Alignment Works

Overbridge

to LLANELLY

Horeb

to LLANELLY

to CYNHEIDRE

Probable original
course of the
Carmarthenshire
Railway or Tramway

Site of
Colliers Halt

to CYNHEIDRE

1960 Re-Alignment
Proposed as tunnel
Rock Cutting Constructed

felinfoel
Siding

Reservoir

Pre 1960
Alignment

Quarry Mawr
Siding

Dam

Pre 1960
Alignment

Probable original
course of the
Carmarthenshire
Railway or Tramway

Felinfoel

to LLANELLY

Quarry Mawr

Possible site of
Reservoir
Construction Siding

to LLANELLY

SCALE – All Plans

0 1 2 3 4 5 6 7 8 9 10   Chains = 1/8 Mile

313

Chapter Twelve
The Cynheidre Branch

The story of the Mynydd Mawr line over the four decades from 1950 to 1990 is entirely dominated by the development and decline of Cynheidre colliery. Trial borings in anticipation of this major project actually began as early as 1949, and by the early 1950s detailed planning was under way. It was envisaged that by the time the pit was fully developed underground it would be possible to raise all the coal produced in the Gwendraeth valley at Cynheidre. Construction of the £7½ million scheme, then described as the largest anthracite mine in Europe, began in March 1954, largely under German direction. At this stage it was anticipated that the new pit would produce 600 tons per day by 1956, with output later rising to 4,000 tons per day. In the event construction took several years whilst mining engineers drove tunnels to connect the new pit below ground with Pentremawr colliery at Pontyberem and Great Mountain colliery at Tumble. The link to Great Mountain No. 3 shaft, originally Cwm or 'Cwm Sinkings', was completed by the end of 1958, and some coal was lifted in 1959. The official opening of Cynheidre colliery eventually took place in November 1960.

Not surprisingly, such an important colliery project had considerable implications for the L&MM route. Initially it was estimated that when Cynheidre was in full production it would require 21 or even 24 trains per day, each comprising 18 wagons. As the existing single line lacked suitable passing loops, it could only handle such traffic by being in continuous use right around the clock. In preference to this, it was suggested that the line's capacity might be increased either by doubling the track between Sandy and Cynheidre, or by electrifying this section to speed the flow of traffic and obviate the need for double track. With all the advantage of hindsight, the second of these notions now seems astonishing – but the very fact that it was put forward is a measure of the promise then perceived in the Cynheidre development.

After further consideration, more modest plans were announced by the Western Region of British Railways in September 1956. The principal features of these proposals were the re-alignment of the single track to ease severe curves and gradients, and the provision of signalling between Old Castle Crossing at Llanelly, and Cynheidre. Instead of doubling the entire section it was now planned to double the line only between Old Castle Crossing and Sandy, and to provide a passing loop at Magpie Grove, just north of Quarry Mawr. These improvements were intended to make the L&MM line fit for use by the heavier and more powerful '42XX' class 2−8−0 tank locomotives of the former Great Western Railway. By introducing these engines it was calculated that trains of 35 wagons would be feasible, consequently reducing the number of trains needed each day to 14 or less. Additional siding accommodation at Sandy and nearby at Sandy Gate was deemed to be necessary, but it was anticipated that the remaining rail facilities afforded to the Llanelly Harbour Trust would be closed on the completion of the new works. A 1939 scheme for improved siding space at Tumble was also laid to rest finally by these developments.

For most of the 1950s the construction of Cynheidre colliery had little effect upon the Mynydd Mawr line and its operation. In the early 1950s the '1901' and '2021' class tank engines were withdrawn, and replaced by the new '16XX' class pannier tanks. Llanelly shed was given a sizeable allocation of these engines, and it became quite common for three to be employed on one train from Sandy up the gradient to Cynheidre. This method of working was well described in an article in *Trains Illustrated* in 1954. In it the author, R.C. Riley, gave an account of a brakevan journey he had made from Sandy to Cross Hands and back in the previous year. The train, comprising 50 empty wagons and 2 brakevans, had been hauled by Nos. 1607 and 1618, with No. 1628 giving banking assistance at the rear. As the train tackled the reverse curves beyond Furnace the leading locomotives were frequently out of sight of the banker and the brakevans. After a halt for water at Cynheidre, the banking engine returned to Llanelly, whilst the other two continued with the train. At Great Mountain colliery 25 wagons were detached, and before the remainder went forward, No. 1618 was attached to the back of the train to facilitate the removal of another 15 wagons for S & R Colliery (Blaenhirwaun). The remaining 10 wagons were taken on to New Cross Hands by No. 1607.

At Cross Hands a long delay ensued whilst No. 1618 marshalled its train from Blaenhirwaun, and worked back to Sandy with a headway of 30 minutes under the time interval system of working. No. 1607 then took charge of seven loaded wagons being sent from New Cross Hands to the Tir John power station at Swansea. A further 13 wagons for assorted destinations were collected at S & R Colliery siding, and at Great Mountain another eight were picked up, in this case for loading onto the S.S. *Canada* at Swansea docks. Although Tumble was the usual place for down trains to take on water, this train evidently took water at Cynheidre. At the same time about one third of the wagon brakes were pinned down, and to avoid any risk of a runaway a further third were pinned down just beyond Horeb. The noise as the train slowly snaked its way downhill may well be imagined, but some of the wagon brakes had to be unpinned to enable the train to clear a short stretch of rising gradient by the Cwmlliedi reservoirs. Eventually the travellers returned to Sandy about five hours after they had set out.

By the late 1950s there were several signs of change at Llanelly. After the closure of the North Dock for commercial traffic it was used for several years for the storage of naval landing craft. These vessels were removed at the time of the Suez crisis of 1956/7, leaving only a few small craft based at the dock. The Peckett tank engines belonging to the Llanelly Harbour Trust were dispersed, and all lines at the North Dock fell into disuse. The connection to the dock from the South Wales main line was recovered on 25th January, 1959. Nearby the Stradey estate railway was also dying. The Old Castle tinplate works was closed in April 1957, and the only traffic on the Stradey line to be worked by Messrs Nevills' saddle tanks was an occasional service from Sandy or Llanelly steelworks down to the Copperworks and the Great Western Dock.

The development of Cynheidre colliery had the effect of putting the other pits served by the railway under notice of closure. These pits provided the reservoir of labour for the new mine, and as production at Cynheidre increased activity at the other pits was gradually cut back. Great Mountain colliery closed on 5th May, 1962, followed three weeks later by New Cross Hands. It was estimated at closure that the annual output lost was 55,000 tons and 63,000 tons respectively. However access to part of the Cross Hands workings was retained through the Cwmgwili drift, situated to the east of the village. In April 1968, these workings were integrated with those of the nearby Lindsay colliery, which was then officially closed. Meanwhile, on the west side of Cross Hands the Blaenhirwaun colliery was shut down on 1st September, 1962. Once again the reason for closure was the transfer of manpower to Cynheidre, although in this case the annual output lost was just 41,000 tons. The end of Blaenhirwaun also put an end to one of the Gwendraeth valley's most remarkable sights – that of one of the small colliery locomotives struggling up the hillside from the pit to the exchange sidings by the L&MM line. Only three loaded wagons were allowed per trip! Inevitably these changes had a bearing on the working of the Mynydd Mawr line.

The working timetable for the summer of 1959 is reproduced, but by 1962 two trips only operated to Cynheidre, and by this time the track realignments proposed in 1956 had been carried out. At Quarry Mawr a new cutting had been blasted out of rock to take the line through hillside west of the original formation. At Horeb the track was substantially realigned for about half a mile, taking the railway away from the original Carmarthenshire Railway route for most of this distance. The most notable feature of the work was the provision of signalling as far as Cynheidre, and the installation of a loop at Magpie Grove capable of taking two diesel locomotives, 45 wagons and a brakevan. Signal boxes were constructed at Sandy, Magpie Grove and Cynheidre in 1960, and were brought into use in July 1962. These developments enabled the heavier '42XX' class 2−8−0 tank locomotives to be used on some Cynheidre trains, and it is believed that '56XX' 0−6−2 tank engines were also tried.

. Although the new colliery quickly became the pre-eminent mine in the Gwendraeth valley, it did not prove to be as spectacularly successful as some had anticipated. Rail traffic was seldom heavy enough to justify all the costly improvements which had been carried out, and when the English Electric Type 3 diesels (later known as class '37') were introduced the working timetable showed no more than three services daily from Cynheidre, with one trip per day from Llanelly to Cross Hands and back worked by a 350 hp diesel shunter. This train conveyed some agricultural traffic, including fertilisers, and house coal, as well as locally produced anthracite. Magpie Grove signal box, which was very little used, is believed to have been closed by 1965, whilst those at Sandy and Cynheidre were closed with effect from 25th February, 1968. The railway then reverted to single token, 'one engine in steam' operation.

The former GWR locomotive shed at Llanelly was closed on 1st November, 1965, but the L&MM line is believed to have been steam-worked right

The pitheads of Cynheidre No. 3 (formerly Cwm or Great Mountain No. 3) photographed in 1987.   *Author*

Cynheidre colliery, a few weeks before the demolition of the winding gear, seen here
14th December, 1989.   *Author*

Carway Fawr drift mine, Cynheidre, near Llanelli, photographed on 14th December, 1989.   *Author*

An interesting view of the trams descending towards the drift entrance at Cwmgwili Colliery, 24th March, 1988.   *Author*

Overgrown course of Waddell's line at Cross Hands seen on 14th December, 1989.
Author

Tramroad route between K&L Canal Co, dam and Cross Hands, 14th December, 1989.
Author

up to this date. Shortly before, in September 1965, a remarkable steam-hauled railtour was organised which provided echoes of the early days of the L&MMR. A special train of empty wagons was assembled to take railway enthusiasts over the whole length of the line from Sandy to Cross Hands hauled by a '16XX' 0–6–0PT. The train returned to Tumble where the passengers alighted before walking down the hill to the terminus of the old BP&GVR at Cwmmawr. The participants then went back to the coast in a train of brakevans hauled by another '16XX' class locomotive. After the closure of its home shed, one of the Llanelly engines, No. 1607, was sold to the NCB for use at Cynheidre colliery. There it saw regular use until a cracked frame caused it to be condemned in 1969.

By 1966 anthracite traffic at the northern end of the line was negligible, and it was felt that the surviving agricultural and house coal traffic could be taken satisfactorily by road. Accordingly the service to Cross Hands and Tumble was ended with effect from 17th October, 1966, and the top two miles of the line were abandoned. The track is believed to have been dismantled by, or in, 1968. Rails were left in position from Cynheidre to a point near Ty-Isha farm, south of Tumble, primarily to allow coal traffic to be worked from the Cynheidre No. 3 shaft ('Cwm sinkings') when required. In practice British Railways made little use of this section, and in 1970 it was transferred to the NCB. The new owners also had relatively little use for the section, and in 1973 it is believed to have been disconnected at a point just north of Cynheidre. Thereafter the track was left to gather weeds, and it is doubtful if it was ever used again. In the summer of 1990 it was alleged that gypsies were quietly removing some of the rails, and burning the sleepers.

In 1966 Llanelly was officially renamed Llanelli, and the new spelling was also adopted for railway purposes. In the early 1970s the track layout at the Llanelli end of the line was simplified further. The L&MM route south of Sandy was reduced to a single track leading into the up South Wales main line, with a headshunt siding adjacent to the junction. Some of the rails of the Stradey estate line remained in situ at Old Castle, but without any connection to the Cynheidre branch. The Old Castle Crossing signal box on the main line (which had replaced an earlier box in 1961) was closed in December 1973. Eventually all signalling in the Llanelli area came under the control of the power signal box at Port Talbot. Even so, one signal box managed to survive some distance from any railway tracks, namely the North Dock box, originally built by the Llanelly Harbour Trust and manned by the L&MMR. Located close to the dock gates, it was used for several years in the 1970s by Corcoran Marine, who piloted small vessels in and out of what was left of the docks. They also arranged unloading facilities for Eastwood Ltd, who leased part of the North Dock for the importation of grain for their poultry business at Pembrey. This modest trade of perhaps 400 tons each month ended in the early 1980s. At about the same period, however, part of the nearby Carmarthenshire Dock was being used by a firm dredging sand in the Burry estuary and Carmarthen Bay.

The 1980s proved to be a difficult decade for Llanelli and district. Less than three years after a costly reconstruction of Llanelli Steelworks by the

A locally organised railtour to Cynheidre about to be flagged away from Llanelli by Denzil Davies MP, in the presence of the Mayor and other dignitaries in May, 1987.   *Author*

Good Friday, 24th March, 1989. The last day of coal traffic from Cynheidre Colliery.
R. Pittard

Duport company, the works was closed quite suddenly in March 1981. The shock in the town was palpable, but protests were to no avail. The Carmarthen Bay power station at Burry Port was closed in 1984, by which time the general economic recession had caused many other redundancies. The year long miners' strike of 1984–85 did nothing to help the coal industry, and by 1987 it was rumoured that even Cynheidre, the showpiece pit of the 1960s, was under threat. As the colliery was soon reduced to working only one coal face the possibility began to look credible, although development work on an entirely new drift adjacent to Cynheidre – Carway Fawr – was well advanced.

Following the closure of the marshalling yard at Llandeilo Junction, east of Llanelli, train crews signed on at Llanelli goods yard. Further cuts brought about the closure of this signing-on point on 4th April, 1988, and responsibility for Cynheidre branch trains was given to Margam men. Whereas in the early 1980s some coal from Betws colliery, Ammanford, had been brought up to Cynheidre for washing, by this time all coal traffic over the line had become more erratic. Indeed, in the summer of 1988 it was reduced to a service at weekends only, taking stockpiled anthracite from Cynheidre to Margam for forward movement to Immingham for shipment. Meanwhile work on the Carway Fawr drift was suspended, allegedly on geological grounds, and in September 1988, it was admitted that the future of Cynheidre was under review. By December British Coal had announced its intention to close the colliery, and although many of the miners wanted to resist the closure, their objections came to nothing.

The last shift at Cynheidre colliery was worked on Good Friday, 24th March, 1989. The final coal train hauled by class '37' diesel No. 37906 left Cynheidre at 10.28 destined, like so many other Mynydd Mawr line trains, for Swansea docks. Soon after a sister locomotive, No. 37718, made two trips up the branch to clear wagons, but within a few hours all traffic had ceased. At Cynheidre itself a small diesel shunting engine and a few wagons were allowed to remain in sidings south of the colliery, in the care of the Llanelli & District Railway Society. Several months later, on 6th September, No. 37207 made a cautious trip up the branch to add a mark 1 brake second coach to the Society's collection. This short excursion helped to clear the way for the Monmouthshire Railway Society's last train on 14th October, described at the beginning of this book. It is surely one of the ironies of the L&MMR's history that although it never ran an official passenger service, both the first train in 1881 and the last train in 1989 were operated for the benefit of passengers.

At the time of writing the Cynheidre branch rests and rusts. The headgear at Cynheidre No. 3 was dismantled in 1989 and the shaft filled; the Nos. 1 and 2 winding towers were demolished in January, 1990. Only the Carway Fawr drift remains, reputedly requiring only a few months work to make it ready for coal production. Some believe that this will only happen when the drift is in private ownership; some doubt if it will ever happen at all. After the closure of Cynheidre, care and maintenance was provided by men from Cwmgwili, near Cross Hands which for some years has employed a small workforce to extract coal from old pillar and stall workings. Early in 1992, however, it was learned that Cwmgwili would close at the end of March,

1992, and responsibility for Carway Fawr would be transferred to Betws colliery at Ammanford, five miles away.

Meanwhile some coal is still worked in the Gwendraeth valley, either being excavated opencast, or mined by Tumble Anthracite Ltd from their drifts at Dynant Fach, near Tumble, one of which actually reaches into the former workings of the Great Mountain colliery. If that provides a reminder of the railway's heyday, the discovery at Gorslas in 1990 of some stone blocks on the alignment of the original Carmarthenshire Railway has provided a reminder of the tramroad era. Local interest has been considerable, not least because the village of Gorslas owes its origins to the tramroad. Accordingly although most blocks have been left in place, a few have been moved to form part of a short length of reconstructed tramroad. This is being laid on a memorial plinth built near the crossroads at Gorslas, which is also near the site of the iron ore levels at the terminus of the tramroad. Tramplates have been cast to fit the blocks, but in the absence of any Carmarthenshire plates, the new plates are based on the pattern used by the nearby and contemporaneous Llangennech tramroad.

This small memorial will be a permanent reminder of the line at its northern extremity. At its southern end there has been discussion in Llanelli over the possibility of preserving the route between Old Castle and Furnace in recognition of the town's historic railway and industrial links. As the line to Furnace dates back to the days of Alexander Raby, the idea is appropriate. However it remains to be seen whether Carway Fawr will ever be worked; the survival of the Mynydd Mawr line to Cynheidre depends upon coal. It was ever thus.

Appendix One

Carmarthenshire Railway – Report to Proprietors, May 1807

Nearly five years having elapsed, since the passing of the act for making the Carmarthenshire Railway, it cannot fail to be interesting to the proprietary to have a concise account of the progress and present state of the concern; as it appears, that, after the expenditure of the original subscription of £18,500, a farther subscription of £6,500, and bonds amounting to £1,500 given under the seal of the Company, the Railway is incomplete by two miles; that the income or tonnage is not more than adequate to pay the current expenses; and, that there is no surplus to divide among the Proprietors.

It is also to be observed, that, in the above expenditure, the late subscription of £2,800 is not included; £2,500 of which is for extending the Dock, and thereby rendering it safe for vessels coming to Llanelly for coals, &c. during the prevalence of the south-western gales, so terrible upon this part of the Welch coast; and £300 is for making that part of the Rail-road from Stradey Furnace to the Flatts double.

The original estimate for making the Rail-road, including the Bason and Wharf, was £18,467: 16s; the returns from tonnage were laid at £5,500 per annum, thus presenting a prospect, and holding out an inducement to persons disposed to subscribe, of very ample returns for the shares they might take in this concern.

In the report of June 28, 1803, and when the General Assembly of August 1, 1803, recommended the second subscription of £6,500, the tonnage was estimated at £7,000 per annum.

The tonnage, arising from the Rail-road, &c. from December, 1805, to December, 1806, was about £900: 15s: 3d;* the current expenses during that time amounted to £1,005: 9s. 10d.

A recital of some of the principal causes of the excess of the expenditure above the estimate, and the present small returns of tonnage, with the suggestion of any measure likely to secure the prosperity of the concern, or, at least, to wind up the outstanding and unsettled accompts [sic], amounting to many thousand pounds, must necessarily engage the serious attention of every Proprietor.

It will be proper to mention, first, the expenses incurred in passing the act of parliament, which were about £1,100.

As the act of parliament authorised the Company to purchase the Rail-road then in use, and belonging to Mr Alexander Raby, the sum of £3,117, or thereabouts, has been debited by Mr Raby, in his accompt with the Company, as the value thereof.

The act of parliament, authorising the making of the Rail-road, describes the place where the Rail-road shall commence, viz. Llanelly Flatts, and also the place where it shall terminate, viz. the Lime Rocks, called, Castell y Garreg; and the course or direction of the Rail-road is laid down in a map or plan, with a book of reference, authenticated by the Speaker of the House of Commons, and from which course or direction it is enacted, the Rail-road shall not deviate, but under certain circumstances therein mentioned.

The course of the Railway actually laid down (upon examination) is found to deviate from the parliamentary course very considerably, and the principal deviation from the parliamentary course is a worse course, and has occasioned an additional expense to the Company of £1,000 or more.

There have also been made from and out of the parliamentary course of the Rail-road, and absolutely unauthorised by the act of parliament, branches to various works of Mr Alexander Raby, at Stradey Furnace and Forge, &c.; these branches exceed 8,700 yards; in addition to which, near the great mountain, there is a branch to a mine of Mr Alexander Raby's, extending 1,614 yards from and out of the main line or parliamentary course.

The expense of making the branches about Stradey-Furnace has amounted to £7,000, and at the Great Mountain to £1,089, and which sums form only a part of Mr Raby's accompt with the Company.

Towards Mr Raby's general accompt, after many thousands had been voted and paid by the Committee, Mr Raby obtained three bonds of £500 each, under the Seal of the Company, at a General Assembly, held July 12, 1805.

In the minutes of that day, it is stated, Mr Raby held forty-two shares, and had proxies from various Proprietors for ninety-six more, making together one hundred and twenty-eight shares: by the act of parliament, one hundred and twenty-six shares constitute a General Assembly.

Justice to several respectable independent Proprietors at Llanelly requires it to be noticed, that the minutes bear strong testimony to their exertions in resisting many improper proceedings, and in requiring the accompts of Mr Raby to be examined, that the true balance might be ascertained; but, notwithstanding their repeated endeavours, they have been unable to effect it, and, it is to be feared, as the Committee is at present constituted, they never will be able.

In the month of August, 1805, several Proprietors, resident in London, having requested information relative to the Rail-road, which was reduced to writing, and transmitted to the Clerk, to be laid before the Committee at Llanelly, the information requested was furnished.

The latter end of the same month (August 1805), a Proprietor from London visited Llanelly; upon whose return to London, it was suggested that the Committee should, in future, consist of Proprietors in London, as well as at Llanelly; this proposal, being

*It is uncertain whether the dock-dues, amounting to about £100, are included in the £900: 15s: 3d.

submitted to the next General Assembly, held at Llanelly, November 7, 1805, was
acceded to.

The Committee of Proprietors, in London, immediately, upon their appointment,
proceeded to inquire into the state of the concern; and, being assisted in their
inquiries by several of the Committee at Llanelly, have obtained the information
which it is now thought proper to communicate to the Proprietors at large.

Among other measures, recommended by the Committee in London to the Committee at Llanelly, was the investigating the accompt of Mr Alexander Raby, an accompt
of such magnitude and importance, as it is to be feared involves in it the ruin or
recovery of the Company's affairs, as far as any profits to the Proprietors are to be
expected.

The Committee in London, from copies of the minutes received from Llanelly,
finding that the Committee at Llanelly had been unable with all their exertions to
bring the accompt of Mr Raby into a train of investigation and settlement, came to the
following resolution, December 6, 1806.

That Mr Druce (a Proprietor), be requested to apply to Mr Raby for the purpose of
obtaining his consent to submitting to arbitration the whole of his accompts, and
particularly the deducting from his accompts the costs and charges of making all and
every branch from the main line (or parliamentary course) of the Rail-road, with every
expense attending thereon, such branches not being within the authority and powers
of the act of parliament.

A copy of this resolution was forthwith handed to Mr Raby: but Mr Raby has not
acceded to this proposal.

It must, therefore, be obvious to every Proprietor, who is desirous of promoting the
welfare of the concern, that some measure must be resorted to, whereby the outstanding accompts of the Company may be forthwith adjusted and discharged, and such
other regulations adopted as may be requisite to complete the whole course of the
Rail-road.

The measure submitted to your consideration is, that the Committee to be chosen,
in future, should consist entirely of Proprietors in London; and, as they have no local
interests at Llanelly, it is presumed that many numerous evils arising from this source
will thereby be removed, and thus the progress and prosperity of the Railway be no
longer impeded.

In proposing this measure, it is expressing the opinion of several respectable
Proprietors at Llanelly, of whose effectual assistance and exertion in carrying into
execution the orders and directions of such a Committee there is little doubt.

Upon the Rail-road being completed, the tonnage will be considerably increased,
and the proprietary may expect to receive some return for the capital they have
advanced.

Signed, by order of the Committee in London,

JOSEPH FEARN,

No. 10, Cornhill,
May 9, 1807.   Acting as their SECRETARY

Appendix Two

Carmarthenshire Railway Notice
and Report, 1844

Thomas Arms, Llanelly, 18th May, 1844.

At a Special General Assembly of the CARMARTHENSHIRE RAILWAY or TRAM-ROAD CO. held this Day in pursuance of the following Notice, having been duly inserted in the Carmarthen Journal News-paper, agreeable to the directions of the Act of Parliament :—

"We, the undersigned being five of the Proprietors of the CARMARTHENSHIRE RAILWAY or TRAM-ROAD COMPANY, each possessed of, or entitled to, two or more shares in the said undertaking, Do HEREBY GIVE NOTICE, That a Special General Assembly, of the said Company of Proprietors, is hereby convened, and will be held on SATURDAY, the 18th day of MAY next, at 12 o'clock at noon, at the THOMAS ARMS INN, in the Town of LLANELLY, in the County of Carmarthen, for the purpose of authorizing the said Company or such person or persons as they may appoint, to treat with, sell and convey to the Commissioners acting in execution of the provisions of an Act of Parliament made and passed in the last session of Parliament, intituled, "An Act to alter and amend an Act for the Improvement of the Navigation of the rivers Burry, Loughor, and Lliedi, in the Counties of Carmarthen and Glamorgan, and to improve the Harbour of Llanelly, in the said county of Carmarthen," for the purposes in the said act specified, the Dock, Reservoir or Channel, Quay and other Walls and Land in immediate connexion with the said Dock belonging to the said Carmarthenshire Railway Company, which said Dock, Channel, and Works, are situated at a place called the Flatts, in the parish of Llanelly, in the said county.

"And also, that the said Special General Meeting is convened, and will be held, to consider and determine upon the propriety of authorizing the said Company of Proprietors of the said Carmarthenshire Railway or Tram-Road Company, their Clerks, Servants, or Workmen to take up and remove the Tram-plates and other Materials and Property of, and belonging to, the said Company, now on or about the Railways or Tram-Roads, Dock, and other Works of the said Company, and to sell or otherwise dispose of the same, and to divide the proceeds of such Sale or Sales amongst the Shareholders or Proprietors of the said Railway or Tram-Road, as may then and there be agreed on.

"Given under our hands this 23rd day of April, 1844,

R. GORING THOMAS,
R. J. NEVILL,
ALEXR. DRUCE,
M. WILLIAMS,
RICHD. NEVILL, JUN."

The following Proprietors attended :—

			Proxies held by R. J. Nevill, Esq.	
David Lewis, Esq.	5 Shares.			
M. Williams, Esq.	5		*Brought forward*	50 Shares.
R. Dunkin, Esq.	6		Alex. Druce, Esq.	27
Henry C. Eaton, Esq.	3		R. Nevill, Jun., Esq.	5
R. J. Nevill, Esq.	8		R. G. Thomas, Esq.	11
Proxies held by R. J. Nevill, Esq.			Chas. Druce, Esq.	7
Exors. of Jas. E. Hammett	2		Exors. of Z. Bennett	18
G. M. Davidson, Esq.	21		T. Starling Benson, Esq.	7
			Richard Rees, Esq.	1
	50			126 Shares.

R. J. NEVILL, Esq., was elected Chairman.

RESOLVED,—

That the Chairman and David Lewis, Esq., be requested and authorized to treat with the Commissioners for Improving the Llanelly Harbour, for the Sale of the Dock and Premises described in the above Notice, subject to the confirmation of such Treaty by the next Special General Assembly of this Company.

That the consideration of the question of the Propriety of the Taking Up and Disposing of the Rails be postponed; and that the Chairman, and David Lewis, Esq., be requested to obtain the opinion of Council as to the legality of taking up the Rails.

That the Accounts now exhibited be printed, and that a copy, together with a copy of these Resolutions, be sent to each Shareholder whose Address and Residence is known.

That a Special General Assembly be convened to be held at the house of Messrs. Charles Druce and Sons, in London, on Monday, the 17th day of June next, at 12 o'Clock at Noon, for the purposes specified in the Notice by which this Special General Assembly was convened.

R. J. NEVILL, CHAIRMAN.

C. N. BROOM, *Clerk.*

No. 389

Llanelly & Mynydd Mawr Railway Co.,

WORKMAN'S PRIVELEGE TICKET.

RETURN.

Between _____

And _____

On _____

Issued to _____ • _____ subject

to conditions printed on back.   [OVER].

WATKINS, LTD., SWANSEA.

Courtesy T. David

Courtesy Kent & East Sussex Railway Co.

Llanelly and Mynydd Mawr Railway.

24th Nov 1921

No. 7652 *A F Stephens* _____ has permission

to ride in the Trucks, Brake-van or Carriage

From *Llanelly* to *Cross Hands*

Single Journey only.
Return

Why given ___ *Available until Dec 31st 1922*

Superintendent.

Appendix Three

The Llanelly and Mynydd Mawr
Railway Act, 1875

Tolls.

32. The Company may demand and take in respect of the use of the railway any tolls not exceeding the following; (that is to say,)

Tolls for goods.

In respect of goods and minerals conveyed upon the railway :

Class 1. For all coals, culm, cinders, cannel, ironstone, iron ore, limestone, chalk, sand, slag, and clay (except fireclay), dung, compost, and all sorts of manure, and undressed materials for the repair of public roads or highways, per ton per mile one penny halfpenny; and if conveyed in a carriage belonging to the Company, an additional sum per ton per mile of one penny :

Class 2. For all coke, charcoal, pig iron, bar iron, rod iron, hoop iron, plates of iron, wrought iron, heavy iron castings, railway chairs, slabs, billets, and rolled iron, lime, bricks, tiles, slates, salt, fireclay, and stone, copper ore, lead ore, tin ore, antimony, and manganese, and all other ores, minerals, and semi-metals, per ton per mile twopence; and if conveyed in a carriage belonging to the Company, an additional sum per ton per mile of one penny :

Class 3. For all sugar, grain, corn, flour, hides, dye-woods, earthenware, timber, staves, deals, and metals (except iron), nails, anvils, vices, and chains, and for light iron castings, per ton per mile threepence; and if conveyed in a carriage belonging to the Company, an additional sum per ton per mile of one penny :

A.D. 1875.

Class 4. For cotton and other wools, drugs, and manufactured goods, and all other wares, merchandise, fish, articles, matters, or things, per ton per mile fourpence; and if conveyed in a carriage belonging to the Company, an additional sum per ton per mile of one penny :

For every carriage, of whatever description, not being a carriage adapted and used for travelling on a railway, and not weighing more than one ton, conveyed on a truck or platform belonging to the Company, sixpence per mile, and a sum of one penny halfpenny per mile for every additional quarter of a ton or fractional part of a quarter of a ton which any such carriage may weigh.

In respect of passengers and animals conveyed on the railway :

For passengers and animals.

For any person threepence per mile; and if conveyed in or upon a carriage belonging to the Company, an additional sum of one penny per mile :

Class 5. For any horse, mule, or other beast of draught or burden, fourpence per mile; and if conveyed in or upon a carriage belonging to the Company, an additional sum per mile not exceeding one penny:

Class 6. For any ox, cow, bull, or head of neat cattle, three-pence per mile; and if conveyed in or upon a carriage belonging to the Company, an additional sum of per mile not exceeding one penny:

Class 7. For any calf, pig, sheep, lamb, or other small animal, twopence per mile; and if conveyed in or upon a carriage belonging to the Company, an additional sum of per mile not exceeding one halfpenny.

33. The toll which the Company may demand for the use of engines for propelling carriages on the railways shall not exceed one penny per mile for each passenger or animal or for each ton of goods, in addition to the several other tolls or sums by this Act authorised to be taken. Tolls for propelling power.

34. The following provisions and regulations shall apply to the fixing of all tolls and charges payable under this Act; (that is to say,) Regulations as to tolls.

A.D. 1875.
———

For all passengers, animals, goods, or minerals conveyed on the railway for a less distance than four miles, the Company may demand tolls and charges as for four miles:

For a fraction of a mile beyond four miles, or beyond any greater number of miles, the Company may demand tolls and charges on animals and goods for such fraction in proportion to the number of quarters of a mile contained therein, and if there be a fraction of a quarter of a mile such fraction shall be deemed a quarter of a mile; and in respect of passengers every fraction of a mile beyond an integral number of miles shall be deemed a mile:

For a fraction of a ton the Company may demand tolls according to the number of quarters of a ton in such fraction, and if there be a fraction of a quarter of a ton such fraction shall be deemed a quarter of a ton:

With respect to all articles, except stone and timber, the weight shall be determined according to the usual avoirdupois weight:

With respect to stone and timber, fourteen cubic feet of stone, forty cubic feet of oak, mahogany, teak, beech, or ash, and fifty cubic feet of any other timber, shall be deemed one ton weight, and so in proportion for any smaller quantity.

Tolls for small parcels and single articles of great weight.

35. With respect to small parcels not exceeding five hundred pounds in weight, and single articles of great weight, notwithstanding anything in this Act, the Company may demand and take any tolls not exceeding the following; (that is to say,)

For the carriage of small parcels on the railway :

For any parcel not exceeding seven pounds in weight, threepence ;

For any parcel exceeding seven pounds but not exceeding fourteen pounds in weight, fivepence ;

For any parcel exceeding fourteen but not exceeding twenty-eight pounds in weight, sevenpence ;

For any parcel exceeding twenty-eight but not exceeding fifty-six pounds in weight, ninepence ;

And for any parcel exceeding fifty-six pounds but not exceeding five hundred pounds in weight, the Company may demand any sum which they may think fit :

Provided always, that articles sent in large aggregate quantities, although made up in separate parcels, such as bags of sugar, coffee, meal, and the like, shall not be deemed small parcels, but that term shall apply only to single parcels in separate packages.

For the carriage of single articles of great weight on the railway :

For the carriage of any one boiler, cylinder, or single piece of machinery, or single piece of timber or stone, or other single article, the weight of which, including the carriage, shall exceed four tons but shall not exceed eight tons, the Company may demand such sum as they think fit, not exceeding one shilling per ton per mile ;

For the carriage of any one boiler, cylinder, or single piece of timber or stone, or other single article, the weight of which, with the carriage, shall exceed eight tons, the Company may demand such sum as they think fit.

A.D. 1875.

36. The maximum rate of charge to be made by the Company for the conveyance of passengers upon the railway, including the tolls for the use of the railway, and for carriages and locomotive power, and every other expense incidental to such conveyance, shall not exceed the following; (that is to say,)

Maximum rates for passengers.

For every passenger conveyed in a first-class carriage the sum of threepence per mile ;

For every passenger conveyed in a second-class carriage the sum of twopence per mile ;

For every passenger conveyed in a third-class carriage the sum of one penny per mile.

37. The maximum rate of charge to be made by the Company for the conveyance of animals, goods, and minerals (except such small parcels and single articles of great weight as aforesaid) on the railways, including the tolls for the use of the railway, and for waggons or trucks and locomotive power, and for every other expense incidental to the conveyance (except a reasonable charge for loading and unloading goods at any terminal station in respect of such goods, and for delivery and collection, and any other service incidental to the business or duty of a carrier, where any such service is performed by the Company), shall not exceed the following sums ; (that is to say,) Maximum rates for animals and goods.

> For everything in Class 1, one penny halfpenny per ton per mile ;
>
> For everything in Class 2, twopence per ton per mile ;
>
> For everything in Class 3, threepence per ton per mile ;
>
> For everything in Class 4, fourpence per ton per mile ;
>
> And for every carriage, of whatever description, not being a carriage adapted and used for travelling on a railway, and weighing more than one ton, carried or conveyed on a truck or platform, per mile sixpence ; and if weighing more than one ton, one penny halfpenny for every additional quarter of a ton or fractional part of a ton which such carriage may weigh :
>
> For every animal in Class 5, fourpence per mile ;
>
> For every animal in Class 6, threepence per mile ;
>
> For every animal in Class 7, twopence per mile.

A.D. 1875.
———

Passengers luggage.

38. Every passenger travelling upon the railway may take with him his ordinary luggage, not exceeding one hundred and twenty pounds in weight for first-class passengers, one hundred pounds in weight for second-class passengers, and sixty pounds in weight for third-class passengers, without any charge being made for the carriage thereof.

Terminal station.

39. No station shall be considered a terminal station in regard to any goods conveyed on the railway unless such goods have been received thereat direct from the consignor or are directed to be delivered thereat to the consignee.

Company may take increased charges by agreement.

40. Nothing in this Act shall prevent the Company from taking any increased charges, over and above the charges by this Act limited, for the conveyance of animals, goods, or minerals of any description, by agreement with the owners or persons in charge thereof, either by reason of any special service performed by the Company in relation thereto, or in respect to the conveyance of animals or goods or minerals, other than small parcels by passenger trains.

Restrictions as to charges not to apply to special trains.

41. The restrictions as to the charges to be made for passengers shall not extend to any special train run upon the railway, in respect of which the Company may make such charges as they think fit, but shall apply only to the ordinary and express trains appointed from time to time by the Company for the conveyance of passengers and goods upon the railway.

Appendix Four

Prospects for Minerals on the Mynydd Mawr, 1876

To

Messrs. The Directors of the Llanelly & Mynydd Mawr Railway Company.

GENTLEMEN,—

Having been requested to report upon the capabilities for the production of Minerals of the District which this line will serve, and after making a careful survey with that view, we beg to report as follows :—

We find at the Upper or Mynydd Mawr end of your line, the existing Collieries known as Gorsgoch and Cross Hands, the former belonging to Mr. B. Jones, Caeffair, Llanelly, and the latter to the Messrs Norton. These Collieries have been in existence and worked for the last 50 years, and have for a part of this time produced at the rate of from 100 to 150 tons per day each. All the seams comprising the lower series of the coal seams on the northern out-crop of the South Wales Coal Basin have been opened upon and proved in this District. The Gorsgoch and Mynydd Mawr Collieries are connected with the Llanelly Railway, by means of which their produce reaches the Port of Llanelly, the distance being 17 miles. On this Railway a locomotive is employed for about one mile on the high ground. The Coal is then let down a self-acting incline plane, and then taken by locomotives from the foot of the same to the Port. The distance from these Collieries by means of your proposed Railway to the Port of Llanelly will be about 13 miles, with an easy descending gradient for the whole distance. Considering the advantage in distance, and the absence of the self-acting incline plane, and of the break caused by such incline, it is but reasonable to anticipate that the larger proportion of the produce of these Collieries will find its way over your line; and the chances are that when a portion of this traffic is diverted over your Railway it will not pay the owners of the Llanelly Railway to incur the expense of a locomotive and other requisite staff and appliances, for a part only of this traffic, hence the probability is that the entire produce of these Collieries will find its way into the market over your line. We think it fair to assume that a quantity equal to 150 tons per day will be carried over the whole length of your line from these Collieries alone. Owing to the absence hitherto of Railway facilities, your line will run from this point to Llanelly through a District the Coal of which is not already opened and developed. The outcrops of the various seams have been proved and can be traced for the whole distance between Mynydd Mawr and Pontyberem, being about 4 miles. The whole of the measures from the Big Vein downwards have been intercepted at Pontyberem, where they prove of full thickness, and are excellent as regards quality. We find from an examination of the sections at Mynydd Mawr, Pontyberem, and at points between these two places, that these seams give a total thickness of 37 feet of workable Coal including the Big Vein and those below. We believe that the best arrangements for the opening and natural development of the minerals of the District would be as follows. :— Leaving Mynydd Mawr the next opening should be at or about Pantgwin, which would be by a slant in the Big Vein and pits into the Pumpquart and lower veins. Such openings would win the Coal under Lord Crawford's farms of Pantgwin, 80 acres; Llanglasnant, 100 acres; and Bryncoch, 120 acres. Also under Mrs. Lloyd's farms of Llechrhodin, 50 acres; and Hirwainolau, 115 acres; Mr. Henry Davies' farm of Tyrlan, 60 acres; Mr. J. T. Jenkins' farm of Llechfedach, 120 acres; and under Blaenhirwain, 80 acres, the property of the late Mr. J. Lloyd Davies: Total area, 725 acres. We estimate that this area contains of workable Coal a quantity equal to 200 tons per day for over 300 Years. Following along the course of the line towards Llanelly the next point for an opening is at the Tumble, which would be by pits, and would win the Coal under Lord Crawford's farms of Danygraig, about 130 acres; Tyrybryn, about 20 acres; Tyissa, 120 acres; and Garnfach, about 30 acres; Mrs. Lloyd's farm of Llettymawr, 90 acres; and under other smaller properties about 20 acres; together making about 410 acres. At the rate of 200 tons per day, we estimate that the Coal under these properties will last upwards of 230 years.

The next point for an opening will be by pits at Pantyffynon. Such pits would develope Sir John Stepney's property, Pantyffynon, 150 acres; Tynywain, 20 acres; Garnfach, 50 acres; Tinton, 40 acres; and other lands 120 acres; together, 380 acres. We estimate the quantity of Coal under these properties to last at the rate of 200 tons per days for upwards of 250 years.

To the north of the line at Pantyffynon and Tumble lie the Dunnant and Cwmmawr Collieries; and the same being within about half-a-mile of your Railway, the chances are that a portion, if not the greater part of the produce of these, will find its way to Market over your line.

The Dunnant Colliery is on the property of Mr. Richard Jenkins of Marchoglwyn, and is worked by Messrs. James Griffiths, Jacob Hughes, and others; and the Cwmmawr Colliery is held by Mr. John Thomas of Court Herbert, Neath, and others.

Next below Pantyffynon your line crosses Llettywilws, the minerals under which belong to Messrs. Watney; Messrs. Astley Thompson and others being the Lessees, who hold the same in connection with the Gwendraeth and Coalbrook Collieries, and who are also Lessees of the minerals under Coedmawr and Cwmblawd, the properties of Mr. W. P. Lewis, Llysnewydd. These Collieries lying within a short distance of your line, a branch or an incline Railway may be inexpensively made, connecting them with your line, the present openings of Messrs. Thompson and others being within half a mile of same. An opening may be made on these properties near your line on the Carway Seams. And although these Collieries are already connected with another line of Railway, we think it likely that a part of their produce may find its way to Market over your proposed Railway. The distance from these Collieries to Port by the present line is about 12 miles, and by your line it would be about 9 miles.

The next point on the line for a Colliery opening is at Bryngwenin, where a slant may be driven to win the two Carway Seams, and would open the Coal under the property of the Rev. Mr. Davies, Llanwunno, about 80 acres; Brynwicked, the property of Mr. R. Jenkins of Marchoglwyn, about 100 acres; Brynhir, the property of Mr. Price Lewis, 140 acres; and under other properties to the extent of about 100 acres; making together 420 acres, yielding a quantity which at the rate of 100 tons per day will last 100 years and upwards.

The next properties are Brynbanal and Penllwynuchaf. Pits here would open the Coal under Sir John Stepney's farm of Brynbanal, 100 acres; Penllwynissaf, (being Glebe land, belonging to Llannon) 60 acres; Penllwynuchaf, the property of Mr. J. Glasbrook of Swansea, 90 acres; and other properties to the extent of about 250 acres, making together 500 acres. These properties would be capable of yielding 100 to 150 tons per day, which would last a long number of years.

We now come to Tynycwm and Disgwylfa. These farms belong to Mr. Johnes of Dolaucothy, and the Coal thereunder is held by Mr. E. Collins, M.P. A Colliery is here opened by a slant on the Big Carway Vein, and its produce now awaits the construction of your line for transit. The area of Tynycwm and Disgwilfa is about 300 acres, and the opening will win of other properties another 150 acres; making 450 acres. The Coal in the seams named under these properties, we estimate equal to yielding 100 tons per day for about 90 years. The lower measures may be won by a shaft sunk on Tynycwm. The Big Vein may be reached at about 50 fathoms. An opening into the lower measures here would win a very large quantity of Coal.

To the north of the line, a little nearer Llanelly, lie the Tynywern, Ffoy, and Tygwyn Collieries, each of which being within three quarters of a mile of your Railway, a part of their produce will in our opinion reach your line for conveyance to market.

We next come to Cynheidref, the property of Mr. Wilson of Bath; Graig, the property of Mr. Buckley; and Brondinni, forming part of the estate in this neighbourhood belonging to Mr. Crawshay Bailey. These properties contain numerous seams of Coal and Fireclay, the produce of which in our opinion, with the facilities afforded by your line, will find its way to Market.

The line here will also receive the produce of the Western part of Sylen Mountain, belonging to the Earl of Cawdor.

Between these last properties and Felinfoel, your line crosses the outcrop of numerous seams of Coal, the produce of which, with the facilities offered, will also find its way to Market over this Railway. The properties belong to Mr. C. W. M. Lewis, Mr. R. G. Thomas, and others.

Having thus indicated our opinions of the capabilities of the District for producing Coal, we will now consider what the chances are as to the working of same. As before stated, we think it reasonable to expect from Mynydd Mawr Collieries 150 tons per day, which would run over (say) 13 miles of your line. From Pantgwyn (say) 100 tons for 12 miles. Tumble, 100 tons for 11 miles. Pantyffynon, 100 tons.

Dunant and Cwmmawr, 50 tons for 10 miles. Bryngwenin, &c, 50 tons. Lletty-wilws and the Pontyberem property (say) 50 tons per day, for 9¼ miles. Brynbanal and Penllwynuchaf (say) 50 tons for 8¼ miles. Tynycwm Colliery, 100 tons per day for 7 miles. Tynywern, Floy and Tygwyn, 50 tons per day, for 6½ miles. Cynheidref, Graig, Brondinni, and Sylen Mountain, 100 tons per day for 6 miles. This would make altogether 900 tons a day; but allowing for some of the Collieries not being fully worked, we are of opinion that in a fair average condition of the Coal Market, a quantity equal to 600 tons per day may be relied upon over an average distance of say 9 miles; and which at 1¼d. per ton per mile will give an annual revenue of £10,125. Taking the working expenses on this income at 50 per cent. there will be left £5,062; or amounting to a return on a capital of £60,000 = 8¼ per cent.

To test the views we have expressed as to probable quantities, we have compared the upper 4 miles of your Railway with the upper 4 miles of the Amman Branch of the Llanelly Railway. We find that these two Districts contain the same seams as near as possible, of equal quality, and they are in other respects similar; and we see no reason, with Railway facilities and time to open, why the upper 4 miles of your line should not produce a larger quantity of Coal than the Cwmamman District, inasmuch as the openings to be made on your line will have the advantage of later experiences as to the best modes of opening, and the Collieries will on your line be placed in a better position having regard to the Railway. And we find, that in fact, the estimate we have made of your upper 4 miles is about that produced by the upper 4 miles of the Amman Valley.

We beg to remain

Your obedient Servants,

WILLIAM WILLIAMS, Mining Engineer, Llanelly
WILLIAM ROSSER, Mining Engineer, Llanelly
JOHN DAVIES, Mineral Surveyor, Llannon

Appendix Five

Col. Druitt's Memorandum to B.O.T., 1911

Memorandum

This railway is generally on a very steep gradient, and there are a considerable number of very sharp curves on it. Several of these are of less than 5 chains radius, and (after consulting Colonel Yorke) I consider that 5 chains is the minimum radius that could be allowed on a line with such steep gradients, and then of course only if the speed is kept very low. I think a maximum speed of 15 miles an hour and 10 miles an hour on the sharp curves of 5 chains is the maximum speed that should be run.

Further none of the curves have check rails at present and all curves of less than 8 chains should be provided with check rails.

Many of the existing double headed rails have been turned and are badly chair-galled and these should be removed, and could be used as check rails and new ones substituted.

The sleepers are generally in good condition and the line is fairly well ballasted.

There are 3 underbridges formed of cast iron girders and these must be renewed by wrought iron or steel girders.

All the siding connections must be provided with bolt locks, and safety trap points provided, which must be connected to a lever, which must be controlled by the Train Staff or Tablet according to the system of working the single line.

Owing to the sharp curves only bogie carriages or short wheelbase carriages should be used not six wheeled carriages.

These must of course be fitted with the continuous automatic vacuum or air brakes.

If platforms are not provided then the carriages must be specially fitted with steps for the use of the passengers.

Platforms are strongly recommended at the termini where there may be a large number of passengers.

Station buildings may be dispensed with but are advisable at the termini.

If a passing place is used on the line it must be provided with the usual signals as required in the case of Light Railways and one of the 3 systems of working single lines approved by the Board of Trade must be adopted.

Col. E. Druitt – 17 June, 1911

Appendix Six

GWR Appendix to No. 10 Section of the Service Timetable for February 1939

LLANELLY AND CROSS HANDS BRANCH.
INSTRUCTIONS FOR DEALING WITH ACCIDENTS ON THE LLANELLY AND CROSS HANDS BRANCH.

The Breakdown Gang is stationed at Llanelly Dock, and when the Gang is required a message must be ser to the Locomotive Foreman's Office, Llanelly Dock, giving full particulars of the derailment, so that it can b determined what equipment, etc., will be required to accompany the vans.

A telephone circuit has been installed on the Llanelly and Cross Hands Branch, and there are instruments ɛ the undermentioned points available for the use of Trainmen in case of emergency :—

      Cross Hands,
      Tumble,
      Cynheidre,
      Felin Foel,
      Sandy.

In cases of accidents occurring between Sandy and Cross Hands causing obstruction of the Running Line, the Guard and Fireman must carry out the Standard Regulations for the protection of their Train, and the preventio of other Trains overtaking them, and the second Guard must telephone to the Inspector or Yard Foreman at Sandy, giving full particulars of the case. If no second Guard is available, the Fireman or Guard, whoever is the nearer must, after protecting the disabled Train, proceed to the nearest telephone for the purpose of telephoning to the Inspector or Foreman at Sandy continuing to exhibit a hand danger signal on the way. The Inspector or Yard Foreman to order out assistance and the Breakdown Gang as above.

A Light Engine with Pilot Guard must be provided to be in occupation of the Running Line between Sandy and the point of obstruction. No Engine of Train must proceed either up or down without the consent of the Pilot Guard on the Light Engine.

The Pilot Guard will pilot the Assistant Engine or Breakdown Train as far as the Guard or Fireman protecting the obstruction at the Llanelly end, and from that point forward the Guard or Fireman protecting the obstruction will act as Pilotman.

In cases of accidents occurring between 6.0 p.m. and 9.0 a.m., the Traffic Inspector at Sandy must be called out, and the Permanent Way Inspector must be advised.

In cases of the Guards being on duty long hours at the point of obstruction, or on Trains in the rear, the Yard Foreman at Sandy, in conjunction with the Inspector at Llanelly Dock, must arrange for the necessary relief to be sent by the Pilot Engine, which will bring the relieved men back to Sandy.

LLANELLY FOUNDRY AND ENGINEERING COMPANY'S SIDING CONNECTION NEAR SANDY SIDINGS, LLANELLY.

Traffic for the Llanelly Foundry Sidings is to be accumulated at Sandy Yard and work to and from there and the Foundry by Pilot trips. Inwards traffic must be drawn from Sandy Yard towards Sandy Gate Exchange Sidings, and propelled from thence into the Foundry Siding and be attached to outwards traffic ; the whole of the wagons must then be drawn out on to the Running Line, the outwards wagons placed on the Sandy Yard side of the connection, and the inwards wagons afterwards berthed in the Foundry Siding.

The outwards wagons will then be propelled to Sandy Yard. The number of wagons so propelled must not exceed 12 at any one time ; the Guard or Shunter in charge m ·t ride on the leading vehicle and be prepared to hand signal to the Driver, or if the leading vehicle is unsuitable f r him to ride in, he must precede the wagons on foot. After sunset a white light must be exhibited on the leading vehicle being propelled.

The key of the Ground Frame operating the above is kept when not in use in a glass case fixed on the wall of the Foreman's Cabin at Sandy Sidings, where the key of the lock securing the catch points on the Stradey Lines near the junction with the B.P. & G.V. Section is also kept.

The catch points key must not be taken from the Cabin by Messrs. Nevills' men unless the key of the Foundry connection is also in the Cabin, and the latter must not be taken away by the Company's staff unless the catch points key is there.

Messrs. Nevills' Engines operate usually once daily over the B.P. & G.V. Section between the junction with the Stradey Lines and Sandy Gate Exchange Sidings. G.W. Engines and Messrs. Nevills' Engines must not occupy this Section simultaneously.

SIDING CONNECTIONS WITH L. & M.M. LINE.

The undermentioned points are equipped with bolts and cotter pins and are normally padlocked in position for movements over the Running Line :—

Felinfoel Mileage Siding	.. .. ..	1 lock, facing for Up Trains. ⎤ Catch points are provided
Quarry Mawr Siding	.. ..	1 lock, facing for Up Trains. ⎬ at these Sidings, pad-
Brick Works, Horeb	.. ..	1 lock, facing for Up Trains. ⎪ locked by octagonal
Horeb Mileage	.. .. ..	1 lock, facing for Up Trains. ⎦ locks.
Each end Cynheidre	.. .. ..	1 lock, facing for Up and Down Trains respectively.
Each end Cynheidre, Mileage Siding	..	1 lock, facing for Up and Down Trains respectively.
Cwmblawd	.. .. ..	1 lock, facing for Down Trains.
Cwm Colliery	.. .. ..	1 lock, facing for Down Trains.
(Also Cwm Colliery Catch Points has an octagonal lock, and the gate a padlock.)		
Each end Railway Terrace Siding	..	1 lock, facing for Up and Down Trains respectively.
Tumble Mileage Siding	..	1 lock, facing for Down Trains.
No. 1 Tank Road, Tumble	..	1 lock, facing for Up Trains.
No. 2 Tank Road, Tumble	..	1 lock, facing for Up Trains.
South end Colliery Connection, Tumble	..	1 lock, facing for Up Trains.
Tank Road, North end, Tumble	..	1 lock, facing for Down Trains.
North end Colliery Connection, Tumble	..	1 lock, facing for Down Trains.
South end Colliery Connection, S.R.	..	1 lock, facing for Up Trains.
North end Colliery Connection, S.R.	..	1 lock, facing for Down Trains.
Cross Hands Loop, South end	..	1 lock, facing for Up Trains.
Cross Hands Loop, North end	..	1 lock, facing for Down Trains.
Cross Hands Loop, Mileage Siding	..	1 lock, facing for Up Trains.

Guards and others, after completion of work at the Sidings, must see that the points are securely locked, and should any of the locks be missing or broken, must report the facts to the Sandy Inspector with the least possible delay.

Two keys have been provided for the use of the Great Mountain Colliery Staff, to enable them to operate the points for the Colliery Engines to travel to and from the Running Line, and the Colliery staff are responsible for securing and padlocking the points in their normal position after use on each occasion. Each Guard working on the L. & M.M. Section has been provided with a key to enable the Company's Engines to have access to the Colliery Sidings, and the Head Guard or Shunter will be responsible for setting the points for the Running Line and for locking them immediately shunting operations in the Colliery Sidings have been completed.

The Cwm Colliery staff have a duplicate key of the special padlock on the gate but not for the octagonal locks on the points and catch point.

FREIGHT TRAINS AND LIGHT ENGINES TRAVELLING FROM SANDY JUNCTION TO OLD CASTLE CROSSING, VIA L. & M.M. LINE.

Drivers of Freight Trains and Light Engines travelling from Sandy Junction, L. & M.M. to Old Castle Crossing (Low Level), G.W.R., must not foul adjacent Lines at the Old Castle Crossing end of the L. & M.M. Up or Down Running Lines, except as follows :—

In the case of Freight Trains or Pilot Trips, the Guard or Shunter in charge must satisfy himself that the Line is clear, and that shunting operations are not being carried out from the Llanelly end of the Sidings before signalling to the Driver to proceed.

In the case of a Light Engine, the Driver must send the Fireman to see that the Line on which it is intended for the Engine to run, is clear as far as Old Castle, where the Engine must come to a stand clear of the fouling point of the two Sidings regarded as the Running Roads, and the Driver must blow two whistles and a crow, and if still detained, the Fireman must proceed to Old Castle Crossing Signal Box.

If shunting is not taking place between the point where the Light Engine is standing, and the connection with the Up Main Line, and if the Signalman is in a position to authorise the Light Engine to draw on to the points, he must give the Driver a green hand signal, but the Fireman will be responsible for seeing that the wagons on adjacent Sidings are clear of the Line on which the Engine is travelling, and that the hand points are in their proper position.

The Driver must not pass the Ground Disc at the points leading to the Up Main Line until it shews the proper indication.

CWMBLAWD MILEAGE SIDING, L. & M.M. SECTION.

A wheel block is provided in the above Siding, and Guards and others concerned will be responsible for padlocking it across the rail after shunting operations have been completed. The lock is of the same pattern as those provided at Siding connections on the L. & M.M. Section, and the instructions issued in regard thereto must be observed.

TRAFFIC FOR HOREB MILEAGE SIDING AND HOREB BRICK WORKS.

Wagons for the above Sidings are usually formed at the rear of Up Trains from Sandy, and berthed by the Assistant Engine.

Sometimes the wagons are taken through to Cynheidre and berthed by a following Down train.

On special occasions a few wagons are propelled from Sandy under the same conditions as operate for traffic to Felin Foel.

NOTICE BOARDS AND LAMP AT CROSS HANDS.

Notice boards, worded as shewn below, are erected, one on either side of the bridge carrying the railway line over the road at Cross Hands :—

On Colliery side of Bridge.
"Shunting movements by Colliery locomotives must not pass this board."
On Llanelly side of Bridge.
"All Up Trains and Engines must be brought to a stand here."

Up Trains or Engines must not pass the board unless and until the Guard of the Train or Fireman, in the case of a Light Engine, has satisfied himself that no conflicting movement is being made by the Colliery Company's locomotive. In the event of the Colliery Company's Engine performing shunting movements at the time, the person in charge of such shunting operation must be verbally instructed that no movement must be made foul of the running Line until the G.W. Train or Engine has passed clear of the fouling point with the Colliery Sidings.

An electric lamp is in use immediately over the notice on the Colliery side of the bridge. This lamp will show a red light towards the Colliery, and towards Llanelly.

FELINFOEL LEVEL CROSSING.

Whistle boards are provided at Felinfoel, one 50 yards North of the crossing for Down Trains, and one 100 yards South of the Crossing for Up Trains.

Drivers must sound their Engine whistles when passing the boards as a warning to users of the level crossing.

INSTRUCTIONS FOR PROTECTION OF LINE DURING BLASTING OPERATIONS—QUARRY-MAWR, BETWEEN FELINFOEL AND HOREB.

The Railway Company will not permit any blasting to be done without permission having first been obtained from the Ganger in charge of the length. An endeavour will be made to restrict the blasting to between the hours of 2.0. p.m. and 3.0 p.m., and a horn or whistle will be sounded as an intimation to our staff that blasting is about to take place, a similar signal being given when it is completed, or the charge withdrawn.

The Ganger of the length must have sufficient notification given to him that blasting is to take place, so as to arrange for the provision of two Flagmen, who must proceed ¾ mile from the quarry in both directions and place three detonators on the Line, and exhibit a hand danger signal. This must be done before any shot is fired.

If all the charges are not exploded, the Quarry Co. must arrange to advise the Company's Ganger, and no Train must be allowed to pass until the charge has been withdrawn or fired.

The Quarry Company will place a man in a suitable position to observe and remove any obstruction that may fall upon the railway lines.

On the signal being given that blasting has been completed, or the charge withdrawn, the Flagmen may remove the detonators from the Line and resume their ordinary duties.

SIDING CONNECTION LEADING TO CAMBRIAN WAGON WORKS, NEAR SANDY SIDINGS, LLANELLY.

The connection is worked by ground levers at each end, which are secured by padlock. The keys of the padlocks, when not in use, must be kept in a glass case in the Foreman's Cabin at Sandy Sidings, where the key securing the catch points on the Stradey Line, near the junction with the B.P. & G.V. Section, and key of the Foundry connection are also kept.

Messrs. Nevill's Engines usually operate once daily over the B.P. & G.V. Section between the junction with the Stradey Line and Sandy Gate Exchange Sidings and Messrs. Nevill's staff must not be given the key of the catch point unless the keys of the Cambrian Wagon Works and Llanelly Foundry connections are in the glass case in the Foreman's Cabin.

The keys of the connections to the Cambrian Wagon Works and Llanelly Foundry must not be taken from the Foreman's Cabin at Sandy unless the key of the catch point in the Stradey Line is in the case.

G.W. Company's and Messrs. Nevill's Engines must not occupy the Section at the same time.

TRIPS BETWEEN SANDY JUNCTION AND SANDY GATE, B.P. & G.V. SECTION.

Wagons not exceeding 30 may be propelled from Sandy Junction, L. & M.M. Section, to the Sandy Gate Siding, B.P. & G.V. Section.

The Guard must ride on the leading vehicle, keep a sharp look-out, and be prepared to hand signal to the Driver, and warn anyone on the Line. If the leading vehicle is unsuitable for the Guard to ride on, or during fog or falling snow, he must precede the trip on foot.

After sunset, fog or falling snow, a white light must be exhibited on the leading vehicle.

Brakes must be applied on the leading vehicles.

TRIPS BETWEEN LLANELLY, NORTH DOCK AND SANDY JUNCTION.

Trips not exceeding 20 loaded or 40 empty wagons may be propelled from Llanelly Harbour Trust Dock via L. & M.M. Section to Sandy Junction, under the personal supervision of the Inspector or Foreman. The trips must be worked by two Guards. The Guard in charge must ride on the leading vehicle, keep a sharp look-out, and be prepared to hand signal to the Driver, and warn anyone on the Line. If leading vehicle is unsuitable for the Guard to ride on, or during fog or falling snow, he must precede the trip on foot.

After sunset, during fog or falling snow, a white light must be exhibited on the leading vehicle.

The trip must be brought to a "dead" stand as soon as the leading portion has passed beyond the G.W. Main Line overbridge where the gradient becomes falling to Sandy.

The Assistant Guard must proceed on foot to Old Castle Level Crossing, and after setting the points and seeing the gates in the proper position, will give a hand signal to the Head Guard. The Head Guard must apply sufficient brakes before proceeding with the trip towards Sandy Junction.

TRIPS BETWEEN SANDY JUNCTION AND FELIN FOEL.

Trips of one Engine load, not exceeding 8 wagons and Brake Van, may be propelled from Sandy Junction to Felin Foel, the Brake Van leading. The Guard must ride in the Brake Van, keep a sharp look-out, and be prepared to hand signal to the Driver and warn anyone on the Line. This working is not permitted during fog or falling snow.

After sunset, a white light must be exhibited on the leading vehicle.

Engines or wagons must not be detached at Felin Foel before the van brake has been applied, and brakes on a sufficient number of wagons next to the Engine have also been applied by the Guard.

The Inspector, or during his absence, the Yard Foreman, will authorise trips to leave Sandy Junction for Felin Foel, but before doing so, all Trainmen must be advised before leaving Sandy, the Guard of the first Down Train afterwards, upon arrival at Cynheidre, must ring up the Foreman at Sandy for permission to proceed from there to Sandy.

After sunset, trips must be worked by two Guards.

OLD CASTLE CROSSING—L. & M.M. SECTION.

During the time that the Gate Attendant at Old Castle Crossing (L. & M.M. Section) is off duty, Assistant Guards or Shunters, or when single-handed, the Guard or Shunter in charge controlling the movements of trips, Trains or Engines, or the Fireman of Light Engines unaccompanied by Guard or Shunter, must see that the gates are properly secured across the public road before permitting movements over the crossing.

The normal position of the gates is across the railway line, and the Gate Attendant's hours of duty are :—

7.0 a.m. to 9.0 a.m.
10.0 a.m. to 1.30 p.m.
2.30 p.m. to 5.0 p.m.

The Yard Foreman will be responsible for locking the gates after the passing of the last Train on Saturdays, and the keys must be kept in the Gate Attendant's Cabin, the door of which is fitted with a Standard Brake Van Lock. The Yard Foreman is responsible for unlocking the gates on Monday mornings.

WORKING ON L. & M.M. SECTION.

Engines of Up Trains must take water at Cynheidre, and those of Down Trains at Tumble. A stop board has been fixed on the Up side of the Line, 305 yards on the Cross Hands side of the Tumble water column, at which Down Trains are to be brought to a stand, and sufficient brakes applied to hold the Train before the Engine or Engines are uncoupled and go forward to the water column for water. After the Engines have taken water and are re-coupled to enable the Train to proceed, the standard incline instructions contained on pages 178 to 180 of the General Appendix must be strictly observed.

A notice board which reads "Speed of Down Trains not to exceed 5 miles per hour," has been fixed on the Down side of the Line, 400 yards on the Cross Hands side of the above stop board to ensure that there would be no difficulty in bringing to a stand, if required, a Down Mineral Train following one the Engine or Engines of which are taking water at the Tumble water column.

INSTRUCTIONS FOR WORKING TRAFFIC TO AND FROM SIDING CONNECTION AT CWM L. & M.M. SECTION.

Arrangements for working traffic to and from the Siding connection at Cwm, L. & M.M. Section, will be made by the Inspector or Foreman in charge at Sandy Sidings, who is responsible for instructing the Trainmen.

Work at the Siding connection must be carried out during the hours of daylight.

The Siding will be served by Up Trains.

Guards of Up Trains performing work at the Siding must apply the Brake Van brake and sufficient wagon brakes in accordance with Rule 151, before the Engine is detached.

TRIPS BETWEEN S.R. COLLIERY CONNECTION AND NEW CROSS HANDS COLLIERY— L. & M.M. SECTION.

Trips worked by two Engines, one in front and one at the rear, must come to a "dead" stand at the South end of Klondyke Loop, which is situated between the connections to S.R. and New Cross Hands Collieries. The leading or Train Engine must then be detached and placed in the Loop, and the rear or Assistant Engine will afterwards propel the Train to the New Cross Hands Colliery Sidings. The Guard must precede the trip on foot, keep a sharp look-out, and be prepared to hand signal to the Driver, and warn anyone on the Line.

Trips to New Cross Hands Colliery may be worked by one Engine in front, this Engine to run around Train if Klondyke Loop is clear.

After sunset, during fog or falling snow, a white light must be exhibited on the leading vehicle.

——————— THE MOUNTAIN BRANCH ———————

INSTRUCTIONS FOR THE WORKING OF THE CROSS HANDS INCLINE.

The following Regulations must be observed by the Inclineman and Hitcher and others concerned in working the Cross Hands Incline.

The Inclineman in charge of the machine at the top of the incline must immediately before each trip satisfy himself, by working the hand-wheel of reversing screw lever, that the brake is in proper working order and can be applied and released without any difficulty, and that the connecting rods have been adjusted. **He must not attempt to adjust the screw connection to alter the travel,** and should any adjustment be necessary an advice to this effect must be at once sent to the Station Master at Tirydail, who will immediately inform the Locomotive Department Foreman, Llanelly, by wire, so that the latter may have the same attended to.

When it is necessary, owing to the wearing of the machine brake, to tighten the same, the man in charge will do this by turning the screw connection at the ends of the brake so as to shorten the screw, **but he must not, under any circumstances, slacken it out or disconnect the rods from the brake strap.** On any difficulty arising, he must at once report it to the Station Master at Tirydail, who will immediately send for the Locomotive Department Foreman, Llanelly.

The machine brake must be worked steadily so as to prevent any jerking or sudden plucking, as otherwise the wagons being inclined may become derailed and the rope be displaced

The Inclineman in charge of the machine at the top must frequently examine the clips through which the rope works, to see that they are in proper position, and he must keep tight all the bolts which fasten the Upper and Lower clips, and change both clips and bolts when necessary. He must also keep all lubricating parts and bearings clean and oiled, with proper machine oil.

The Inclineman must keep a constant look-out to see that the wire rope, chains, shackles, sheaves, poppets, also the points forming the partings midway on the incline, are in order. The Hitcher at the foot of the incline must see that all points there are in good working order. Any defects must be at once reported to the Locomotive Department Foreman, Llanelly, and the Inclineman must not attempt to do anything that requires the attention of a Blacksmith or a Carpenter.

This instruction does not relieve the Locomotive Department Foreman, Llanelly, of any responsibility, and he must act in every respect in accordance with the Company's Rules and Regulations.

The Inclineman and Hitcher must see that the couplings of all wagons to be inclined are in such a position as to prevent their striking the sheaves when being inclined.

The wheel stop-block at the top of the incline must always be kept across the rails until the wagons to descend are coupled to the rope, and the Inclineman has ascertained from the Hitcher at the foot of the incline that the wagons to ascend are ready coupled to the wire rope at the foot. After the descending wagons have arrived at the foot of incline, they must not be detached from the rope until the Hitcher at the foot has been advised by the Inclineman at the top that the ascending wagons have been landed there and have passed the wheel stop-block, and that the wheel stop-block has been placed across the rails.

Between the throw-off points and wheel stop-block at the top of the incline, the wagons must be worked by means of the brakes, and, if necessary, sprags, by the Inclineman at the top, who is responsible for the duty being properly done. No wagons must be allowed to remain on the Line between the throw-off points and the stop-block, excepting those forming the Up or Down trip. The throw-off points at the top must always remain open except when wagons are passing over them.

During inclining operations the points at the foot of the incline must be set in their normal position, namely, for the dead-end Siding.

Whenever possible, all wagons must be double coupled.

Any wagon with a defective or weak brake must not be allowed to travel over the incline, but must be kept back for repair or adjustment and the Locomotive Department immediately advised.

Wagons found to be defective at the summit of the incline must be dealt with as follows :—

    Colliery wagons.—To be returned to Colliery for attention.

    G.W. wagons.—To be taken to Lamb Siding for attention.

Twenty ton wagons may be dealt with over this incline, and the maximum loads for Up and Down Trips are :—

Up.	Against.	Down.
2 empty 12 ton wagons ..	⎱	2 loaded 12 ton and
and 1 empty 10 ton wagon or ..	⎰	1 loaded 10 ton
3 empty 12 ton wagons ..		
3 empty 12 ton wagons	2 loaded 20 ton.	
2 empty 20 ton wagons	2 loaded 20 ton.	
1 empty 20 ton and ..	⎱	1 loaded 20 ton and
1 empty 20 ton or 12 ton wagons ..	⎰	1 loaded 10 ton or 12 ton wagon

The load must not, in **any** circumstances, exceed **2-20 ton** wagons of coal, **or their equivalent.**

The Inclineman at the top must agree with the Hitcher at the foot of the incline as to the balance required to ensure safe inclining. The load must not, under any circumstances, exceed two 20 ton wagons of coal on the Down trip against two 20 ton empty coal wagons on the Up trip. If these wagons are not available for either the Up or the Down trip, the loads must be regulated accordingly, e.g. 2 loaded 12 ton coal wagons Down against 2 empty 12 ton coal wagons Up or equivalent thereto.

When the maximum loads are being operated, the wagons on the Down trip must be braked, and if necessary the brake levers on the empty wagons must be dropped on the rack ; the Inclineman will be responsible for instructing the Hitcher as to the requirements in this connection.

When two loaded 20 ton wagons are balanced by two empty 20 ton wagons, brakes must be applied on all four wagons.

WORKING ARRANGEMENT WITH THE EMLYN COLLIERY CO. ON CROSS HANDS BRANCH

The Emlyn Colliery Company by arrangement with this Company are permitted to work wagons by their own Engine over the Cross Hands Branch, between the junction with their Emlyn Colliery Siding and the Throw-off Points near the top of the incline, and the G.W. traffic to and from the Mileage Siding.

Wagons must not be allowed to remain on the Running Line.

In coming from the Colliery or Mileage Siding, **the Train must be brought to a dead stand at the Emlyn Junction with this Company's Line,** and it may then be drawn down cautiously as far as the Throw-off Points near the top of the incline if the Line is clear to that point, where, after the Inclineman has satisfied himself the wagons brought down are sufficiently secured by means of the brakes, and if necessary, sprags, the Engine may be detached and turned into the Loop.

The Engine must not be allowed to bring more than 8 wagons in fine dry weather and 6 wagons in frosty or damp weather from the Colliery or Mileage Siding at one time, and the person in charge is held responsible for satisfying himself that sufficient brakes and sprags are used, **as will ensure the Train being brought to a dead stand at the Emlyn Junction with this Company's Line.**

Under no circumstances must the Engine be permitted to propel wagons beyond the Throw-off Points on the top of the Incline.

Between the Throw-off Points and the wheel stop-block on top of incline, the wagons must be worked by means of the brakes, and if necessary, sprags, by the Inclineman who is responsible for the duty being properly done.

After each day's work is finished, the Inclineman must personally close and padlock the Emlyn Colliery Junction Points for the safety Siding, and he will be held responsible for the safe custody of the key.

The end of the line for the L&MMR. The railtour special stands just short of the overbridge at Cynheidre, while the 0–4–0 diesel shunter belonging to the Llanelli & District Railway Society idles in the siding nearby on 14th October, 1989.		*Author*

Appendix Seven
Some Standard Gauge Industrial Locomotives Associated with L&MMR

1. *Blaenhirwaun Colliery, Cross Hands, Carms.*
   (ex New Blaenhirwaun Anthracite Collieries Ltd; N.C.B. from 1/1/1947)
   Colliery Branch closed August 1962.

Name	Type		Builder	Maker's No.	Built	Notes	
LENA	0–6–0ST	OC	AE	1543	1908	(a)	(1)
–	0–6–0ST	OC	AE	1575	1910	(b)	(2)
JOHN	0–6–0ST	OC	AE	1893	1921	(a)	(3)
TONY	0–6–0ST	OC	HL	3457	1921	(a)	(4)

(a) ex New Blaenhirwaun Anthracite Collieries Ltd, with site, 1/1/1947
(b) ex Hook Colliery; /1950

(1) to G. Cohen, Stanningley, Yorks. c.1948
(2) to Great Mountain Colliery, c.1953, (between 7/1950 and 8/1953)
(3) to Trimsaran Colliery, c.1954, (between 6/1954 and 9/1956)
(4) to Cynheidre Colliery, c.1962, (between 5/1962 and 7/1963)

2. *Cross Hands Colliery, (New Cross Hands Colliery), Cross Hands, Carms.*
   (ex Amalgamated Anthracite Collieries Ltd; N.C.B. from 1/1/1947)
   Closed 5/1962.

Name	Type		Builder	Maker's No.	Built	Notes		
N.C.B. No.2	0–4–0ST	OC	CF	1202	1901	(a)	Scr. /1964	
		rebuilt Ridley & Young						
EDITH	0–4–0ST	OC	HC	894	1909	(b)	Scr. /1964	
–	4wVBT	VCG	S	9572	1954	(c)	(1)	

(a) ex Amalgamated Anthracite Collieries Ltd, with site, 1/1/1947
(b) ex Cwmgorse Colliery, c.1950; to Trimsaran Colliery, /1954; Returned c.1955
(c) ex Cynheidre Colliery, c.7/1962

(1) to Graig Merthyr Colliery, Glam. c.1967

3. *Cynheidre Colliery, Five Roads, Carms.*
(Opened by N.C.B. c/1958; Use of standard gauge locos ceased from 1987. Colliery closed 3/1989.

Name	Type		Builder	Maker's No.	Built	Notes	
71516	0–6–0ST	IC	RSH	7170	1944	(a)	(4)
(GLANTAWE)	0–4–0ST	OC	AB	1108	1907	(b)	Scr. c/1965
–	4wVBT	VCG	S	9569	1954	(c)	(3)
–	4wVBT	VCG	S	9572	1954	(d)	(1)
–	0–6–0DH	310hp	S	10072	1961	(e)	(2)
TONY	0–4–0ST	OC	HL	3457	1920	(f)	(3) Scr.
PANTYFFYNNON	0–6–0ST	OC	AE	1507	1906	(g)	Scr./1966
1607	0–6–0PT	IC	Sdn		1949	(h)	(3)
–	0–6–0DH		EEV	D1198	1967	(i)	(6)
–	0–6–0DH		EES	8428	1963	(j)	(7)
520/7	0–6–0DH		EEV	D1199	1967	(k)	(5)
APG No. 1	0–6–0DH		EEV	D1138	1966	(l)	(8)

(a) ex NCBOE, Widdrington Disposal Point, Northumberland, 1/1959
(b) ex Clydach Merthyr Colliery, Glam., 3/1961.
(c) ex Trimsaran Colliery, c.12/1960, (between 7/1960 and 3/1961).
(d) ex Great Mountain Colliery, c.12/1961, (between 8/1961 and 5/1962).
(e) ex Ogilvie Colliery, Glam., 4/12/1962, demonstration loco.
(f) ex Blaenhirwain Colliery, c.1962, (between 5/1962 and 7/1963).
(g) ex Pantyffynnon Colliery, 4/1965.
(h) ex BR(WR), 1607, 21/9/1965.
(i) ex Garw Colliery, Glam., 7/1971; to BR, Canton (for repairs) 12/1977; retd 12/1977; to BR, Canton (for repairs) 7/1981; retd 10/1981.
(j) ex Onllwyn Colliery, Glam., c.5/1968.
(k) ex Brynlliw Colliery, Glam., 10/1983.
(l) ex Pantyffynnon Colliery, 6/1985.

(1) to New Cross Hands Colliery, c.7/1962.
(2) to Moor Green Colliery, Notts., 28/2/1963.
(3) Scrapped on site by Cohen, 9/1969.
(4) to Graig Merthyr Colliery, Glam., 10/1976.
(5) to Pantyffynnon loco shed, 7/1987.
(6) to Maesteg C.P.P., 6/1987.
(7) to Merthyr Vale, 9/1987.
(8) Scr. on site by M.R.J. Phillips, Llanelly, 12/1988.

Locomotives – Gauge 4 ft 8½ in. – stored for Llanelli & District Railway Soc.

Name	Type		Builder	Maker's No.	Built	Notes
102 2751	0–4–0DM	165hp	RH	418790	1958	(a)
520/7	0–6–0DH		EEV	D1199	1967	(b)
LD 1	0–4–0DE		BT/WB	3097	1951	(c)

(a) ex British Coal Opencast, Cwmmawr Disposal Point, Tumble, 5/1988.
(b) ex British Coal, Wernes Landsale Yard, Pantyffyman.
(c) ex B.S.C., Velindre, Llangyfelach.

4. *Great Mountain Colliery (Nos. 1 & 2)*
(ex Amalgamated Anthracite Collieries Ltd; NCB from 1/1/1947).
Colliery closed for winding 28/4/1962.

Name	Type		Builder	Maker's No.	Built	Notes	
JOHN WADDELL	0–6–0ST	OC	HC	912	1912	(a)	(2)
DAVID	0–6–0ST	OC	AB	1786	1923	(a)	(4)
No. 3	0–6–0ST	IC	P	1633	1925	(a)	Scr. c10/1959
–	4wVBT	VCG	S	9572	1954	New 5/54	(3)
–	0–6–0ST	OC	AE	1575	1910	(b)	(1)

(a) ex Amalgamated Anthracite Collieries Ltd, with site, 1/1/1947.
(b) ex Blaenhirwain Colliery, c.1953.

(1) to Felin Fran Colliery, Glam., c.8/1954.
(2) to Morlais Colliery, c.1959.
(3) to Cynheidre Colliery, between 8/1961 and 5/1962.
(4) to Graig Merthyr Colliery, Glam., c.1966.

5. *Llanelly Harbour Trust, Llanelly*
North Dock.

Name	Type		Builder	Maker's No.	Built	Notes	
GLADYS	0–4–0ST	OC	P	812	1900	New 3/00	(3)
No. 2	0–4–0ST	OC	P	813	1900	New 3/00	(2)
No. 1	0–4–0ST	OC	BWN	43202	1916	(a)	s/s
No. 3	0–4–0ST	OC	P	1566	1921	New 11/21	(4)
No. 4	0–4–0ST	OC	P	1646	1930	New 2/30	(1)

(a) ex ROD, 33.

(1) used as hire loco after /1933; to J. & P. Zammitt Ltd, Llanelly, /1951.
(2) to British Insulated Callender's Cables Ltd., Prescot, Lancs., WAVELL.
(3) to R. Thomas & Co.; later WD; later Sharpness Docks, Glos.
(4) to B.C.S. (Engineers) Ltd, Taffs Well, Glam., /1951.

Drifts into the Grass Vein at the Dynant Fach mine, Tumble, owned by Tumble Anthracite Ltd. The course of the Llanelly & Mynydd Mawr Railway is marked by a line of trees on the hillside in the distance; May 1991.   *Author*

Sources and Bibliography

Most of the primary source material relating to the Carmarthenshire Railway and the Llanelly & Mynydd Mawr Railway is to be found at the Public Record Office at Kew, under RAIL 376 and RAIL 1057. Much useful information on the Parliamentary history of these undertakings and on abortive railway schemes is available at the County Record Office in Carmarthen, which also houses numerous relevant documents, most notably the Mansel Lewis papers, and the Stepney Estate papers. Llanelli Public Library also has some original material concerning the Carmarthenshire Railway.

Both the National Library of Wales, Aberystwyth, and the Llanelli Public Library have extensive collections of local newspapers. For the purpose of this study *The Cambrian* of Swansea (1804–1863) and the *Llanelly Guardian* (1863–1953) have been most frequently consulted, although the *Llanelli Star* has been helpful in relation to recent events.

Over the years several magazine articles have been published describing the Llanelly & Mynydd Mawr line. These may be summarised as follows:

GWR Magazine vol.35, 1923, p.155
Trains Illustrated vol.7, 1954, p.472 – J. Bourne, and R.C. Riley
Railway World vol.17, 1956, p.320 – W. Jones
Journal of S.E. Wales Industrial Archaeological Society vol.2 (2), 1976, p.92
   – R.E. Bowen

Llanelli Borough Council has an excellent reputation for its support for the thoughtful study of local history, and a wide range of local literature is to be found at Llanelli Public Library. Secondary sources consulted in the preparation of this book have included the following:

Old Llanelly – John Innes (1904)
The Anthracite Coal Industry of the Swansea District – A.E.C. Hare (1940)
Reminiscences of a Civil Engineer – R. Brodie (1945)
The Canals of South Wales & the Border – C. Hadfield (1960)
Memoirs of Tumble from 1896 – W. Timbrell (1974)
The Burry Port & Gwendraeth Valley Railway Company – R.E. Bowen
   (1976)
Coal Mining in the Llanelli Area, vol.1 – M.V. Symons (1979)
A Llanelli Chronicle – comp. G. Hughes (1984)
Coal Dust and Dogma – G. Anthony (1987)
Remembrance of a Riot – J. Edwards (1988)

Those readers who may have a special interest in the route of the railway and its layout are advised to see Section 57 in the splendid, but specialised, series *Track Layout Diagrams of the GWR and BR, WR* by R.A. Cooke. Section 57 was published in 1985.

Index

d = diagram, p = picture.